Labor
Displacement
and Public Policy

Labor Displacement and Public Policy

Philip L. Martin
University of California, Davis

LexingtonBooks
D.C. Heath and Company
Lexington, Massachusetts
Toronto

Library of Congress Cataloging in Publication Data

Martin, Philip L., 1949–
    Labor displacement and public policy.

    Includes index.
    1. Layoff systems–United States. 2. Insurance, Unemployment–
United States. 3. Supplemental unemployment benefits–United States.
4. Trade adjustment assistance–United States. I. Title.
HD5708.55.U6M37 1982   362.8'5   82–48099
ISBN 0–669–05969–2

Copyright © 1983 by D.C. Heath and Company

Published simultaneously in Canada

Printed in the United States of America

International Standard Book Number: 0–669–05969–2

Library of Congress Catalog Card Number: 82–48099

For Cecily

Contents

Figures and Tables

Foreword

Unemployment is at its highest level in four decades. Many of the unemployed in the United States are experienced workers displaced by plant closings and technological changes. Current economic policies and the changing world economy promise even more labor displacement and unemployment.

In the 1970s, unemployment insurance (UI) protection was extended to cover almost all wage and salary workers. In addition, organized workers in the auto, steel, and other basic industries negotiated or improved supplemental unemployment benefit (SUB) programs. Workers and employers in the printing trades, in shipping, and in the railroad industry adopted programs to assist groups of workers displaced by technology and mergers. UI, SUB, and negotiated displacement agreements continue to be the principal means of assisting laid-off and displaced workers.

The 1970s also saw the rise of special protection programs (SPPs) that provided extra assistance to groups of laid-off and displaced workers. In fiscal year (FY) 1981, the twenty federal SPPs added about $4 billion to the nation's $20 billion UI outlay. SPPs are controversial because they distribute benefits to politically powerful unemployed workers who can trace their unemployment to a federal action. The Reagan administration reduced SPP benefits sharply in FY 1982.

Philip Martin's book examines the evolution of private and public job protections in the United States and Western Europe. It criticizes proliferation in the 1970s of SPPs and cutbacks in the 1980s in SPP and UI benefits. It argues that U.S. policy must be based upon the principle that workers are a fixed cost of production and that management must be more sensitive to the employment consequences of lay-off decisions.

U.S. employers have the right to discharge most nonunion workers at will. U.S. managers believe that production can be efficient even if individual workers have no job security or loyalty to a particular firm. These managers believe that the UI and SPP programs should be changed to force unemployed workers to adapt and to accept new jobs quickly.

Achieving production flexibility by making labor a variable cost may prove a Pyrrhic victory for the U.S. economy. A policy that makes workers easy to hire and fire is a two-edged sword. Management reduces production costs quickly in a business downturn, but workers do not develop the bond to an employer that encourages worker identification with the enterprise and participation in production decisions. In today's information economy, a loyal worker willing to share his knowledge of how to solve production problems is an asset that should be hoarded, not flung into the labor market capriciously. Treating workers as interchangeable parts of the production process denies workers and managers the sense of loyalty and participation that would benefit both.

Philip Martin's book suggests several policies that would begin to convert workers into full production partners. Mandatory advance notice, generous and extended UI benefits, and worker-management committees to discuss and to plan lay-offs would begin to foster the sense of participation that workers, management, and the economy need to compete in today's highly competitive international economy.

Ray Marshall
University of Texas, Austin

Preface and Acknowledgments

U.S. workers are threatened with unemployment from both traditional labor-displacing changes and unprecedented structural shifts in the U.S. economy. Changes in consumer preferences, in technology, and within organizations displace workers. Changes in government policies, such as lower tariffs followed by increased imports, can cause some firms to reduce or cease production and lay off their workers. Recent structural changes that have accelerated the pace of economic dislocations include higher energy costs, the increased sensitivity of U.S. markets to foreign events, and environmental regulations that affect production.

Two basic policy options are available to cope with labor-displacing change: to preserve jobs by helping employers to continue their operations without layoffs; or to permit (even encourage) economic change and aid displaced individuals. Economists argue that changes should be encouraged which promote economic efficiency—maximum output and productivity. Resistance to change is reduced if effective and equitable assistance is available to workers hurt by it.

Labor-displacing change need not mean catastrophe for workers. Most workers made jobless by economic change are eligible for weekly unemployment insurance benefits. Some laid-off workers are entitled to extra public and private benefits. Workers displaced by government actions sometimes receive cash-assistance and adjustment services if they can prove a policy decision caused their dismissal. Many unions are able to negotiate supplemental unemployment benefits for laid-off workers and/or compensation for labor-displacing technological and organizational changes. A few firms give advance notice of dismissal and some provide severance pay.

The integrity of the federal-state unemployment insurance system is threatened by the proliferation of special adjustment-assistance programs for selected groups of displaced workers. The sixteen federal adjustment-assistance programs spent $3 billion to compensate displaced workers in FY 1981, adding 15 percent to the nation's $20 billion UI bill. The United States must make a choice—should we continue adding special protection programs for deserving displaced workers or should we reform the UI system to better cope with all economic change and make special protection programs unnecessary?

This book examines the proliferation of special protection programs. Its thesis is simple. The United States is adding expensive categorical assistance programs that will make UI a two-tiered system, giving extra benefits to the deserving unemployed. Each special protection program has its own criteria for determining eligibility, the amount, form, and duration of benefits, and funding mechanisms. Recognition of the pervasive government role in the economy will lead to more displacement situations where it is alleged that government caused unemployment and to demands for new SPPs.

The inequities of diverse SPPs will generate pressure for comprehensive unemployment assistance to eliminate the need for expensive, selective, and administratively complex categorical programs. But just as the present categorical welfare system continues to defy comprehensive reform, it will be difficult to coordinate SPPs and the basic UI system.

The UI system should be reformed now to make some of the benefits granted to a few unemployed workers by SPPs available to all the unemployed. SPPs should be phased out. Specifically:

1. UI benefits should be increased so that unemployed workers get 60 percent of their average net weekly earnings during the previous year.
2. Eligibility criteria for UI should be uniform in all states.
3. Regular UI benefits should be available for at least twenty-six weeks. Workers laid off because of government decisions should be entitled to additional UI and retraining and relocation assistance.
4. Firms anticipating permanent dismissals should give at least six months advance notice to their employees, relevant unions, and to local employment service offices.
5. Joint industry, labor, and government committees should work with local communities to promote retraining and local job creation.
6. Firms should be discouraged from frequently laying off workers for short periods. UI taxes should be raised to penalize excessive turnover, and UI funds should be used to subsidize workers on short-time (working twenty to thirty hours weekly).
7. Work sharing—two or more part-time workers filling one full-time job— should be encouraged for those workers preferring part-time work to full-time unemployment.

Advance notice and joint consultation are low-cost assistance policies whose effectiveness will vary with local leadership and economic conditions. Increased UI benefits, uniform eligibility criteria, and extra retraining and relocation assistance are expensive additions to a currently unwieldy system. Increasing UI benefits and phasing out SPPs may cost the UI system an additional $4 billion annually. However, this additional UI assistance is a small price to pay given the alternatives—accepting a rapidly evolving and costly two-tiered UI system or limiting UI assistance and then coping with more worker resistance to efficiency-increasing change.

Since this study was completed, the Reagan administration has chosen the second option, limiting UI assistance and sharply curtailing SPP benefits. This strategy may enable the federal government to save assistance dollars in the short run, but penurious treatment of today's unemployed is likely to be a

Pyrrhic victory in the search for rapid economic growth. Workers threatened with unemployment will resist the technological and organizational changes that they accepted in the past, forcing hundreds of employer and worker representatives to bargain over preserving jobs rather than planning for change and growth. In addition to the personal hardships that may accompany the current attitude of niggardly assistance for unemployed, the strategy is likely to backfire.

The reform recommendations suggested in this book are not new. A decade ago, when there were only two significant SPPs, Merrill Murray reviewed the fragmentation of UI programs and recommended that UI benefits be increased and eligibility criteria be liberalized, "making unnecessary such special programs as Trade Readjustment Allowances and Disaster Unemployment Assistance" (M. Murray, *Income for the Unemployed* [Kalamazoo: Upjohn Institute: 1971] p. 61). We cannot continue to defer beneficial UI reforms because of their short-run costs.

Acknowledgments

This book had its genesis in discussions with Howard Rosen and Ellen Sehgal of the U.S. Department of Labor. The National Council on Employment Policy awarded a grant to examine public policies toward labor displacement. The reviewers of the manuscript—Howard Rosen, Sar Levitan, Ellen Sehgal, and Marcia Friedman—offered suggestions that were included in a revision supported by a University of California Faculty Research Grant. A German Marshall Fund grant supported the preparation of chapters 1, 5, and 6. Scott Thomas carefully read the entire manuscript, and Pauline Lindsay typed it.

1   Introduction

Change is inevitable in a dynamic society. Every change divides the population into three (often overlapping) groups: those helped, those hurt, and those not affected directly. Most market economies erect rules to favor the disruptive agents pressing for economic change because the search for profit is thought to increase economic efficiency, defined as the greatest amount of goods and services that can be produced with a country's scarce resources. Change occurs when beneficiaries persuade or force losers to accept it.

Economic theory has long argued that flexible societies are the most productive. A flexible society needs signals to tell producers what to produce and to help consumers decide what to buy. The best guides are prices that reflect the marginal cost of the last unit produced or employed; the cost of producing the next car, the wage of the next worker, the interest cost of the next $1,000, or the rental cost of additional space. In a truly efficient economy, ever-changing prices that reflect production costs guide the constantly changing behavior of informed and flexible people and businesses.

Even though individuals are scurrying to adjust to ever-changing prices, the market economy generates a series of equilibria or resting points. At these moments, everything is in harmony: supply equals demand. The method of comparative statics searches for these resting points and usually finds that a market economy is driven, like the Hegelian dialectic, upward on the road to maximum output. Economists are aware of the numerous real-life departures from this idealized system but still argue that the economy tends toward the equilibria predicted by this price-based theory.

A market economy is meant to benefit consumers, the decision makers whose buying choices set all the changes in motion. But consumers have split personalities. Changing commodity prices may help consumers make buying choices, but they also affect the wages, profits, and rents consumers receive. Since most people seem to prefer stability to flexibility in their own incomes, a variety of institutions and rules exist to modify the changing prices that guide the system. These modifications permeate modern economies, but this book's special concern is the labor-market mechanisms that protect workers from abrupt job loss.

Changing wages play the same role in the labor market that changing prices play in the product market. In theory, a worker should take both the wage and prospects for dismissal into account before accepting a job. This book's examination of private and public responses to labor displacement begins with the caveat

1

that a substantial body of economic doctrine argues that programs and rules to compensate workers for involuntary job loss are misguided because the informed worker already has (or should have) taken the probability of displacement into account before accepting the job from which the employee has been dismissed.

Economic changes displace labor in several ways. Consumer preferences, shaped by tastes, prices, and advertising, determine the demand for particular goods and services. As consumer demands change, so do the combinations of capital and labor needed to produce newly popular goods. The death of a fad often causes labor displacement. For example, the decline of Hula Hoops led to worker lay-offs, just as the popularity of the auto hastened the demise of the blacksmith. Changing consumer demands make job changes inevitable for many individuals. Although individual hardships often accompany such job changes, the U.S. economy usually provides jobs in expanding firms to displaced workers. Some workers suffer a loss of status (from supervisor to worker), but because expanding industries usually pay higher-than-average wages, few workers suffer prolonged earnings losses.

The most studied form of labor displacement is that arising from technical change in production processes. Changes in production methods permit the same output to be produced with less labor and improved capital. Alternatively, technological changes can permit more output to be produced with the same (labor) inputs.

Most technical changes spread slowly. Most labor-saving innovations diffuse in an S-pattern: risk takers quickly adopt the new technology, and their extraordinary (Schumpeterian) profits encourage the mass of producers to follow. Eventually, innovation adoption levels off. Some innovations are adopted by almost all producers while others are confined to a fraction of potential adopters.

Technological changes can simultaneously displace labor, change skill requirements, and create new jobs. Machines that replace labor in one sector (agriculture) can create jobs in another (machine production). If technological change lowers production costs and output demand is elastic (sensitive to price change), total demand for the now cheaper good may increase enough to expand employment despite the labor-saving innovation.

Most economies go through two massive labor shifts inspired by changing production technologies.[1] In the United States, labor shifts from agriculture to industry have reduced U.S. farmers and farmworkers from 95 percent of the population in 1790 to less than 5 percent today. The second shift, from industry to services, is well underway in the United States. Only 20 million U.S. workers remain in goods-producing industries, while 60 million now provide a variety of services. These major employment changes have occurred over relatively long periods.

Structural Changes and Uncertainty

Structural changes that displace labor promise to accelerate in the next two decades. Regional job shifts, persistently high unemployment, and an aging work force promise increased adjustment difficulties. The response of labor, industry, and government will determine the impacts of structural change on employment and economic efficiency. Public policies can help keep workers employed by discouraging lay-offs and dismissals, or they can encourage change by providing generous assistance to reduce the resistance of workers and employers.

Structural changes are not easily predicted. The major forces now reshaping the economy are higher energy costs; an increased U.S. dependence on international markets; continued technological changes, especially as micro-chip computer technologies replace production workers; and the effects of noneconomic environmental, health, and safety regulations on production processes. Persistent inflation may also influence structural change by altering firm investment and consumer-buying decisions. The results include shorter product cycles, more production uncertainty, and less job security.

Real energy costs quadrupled in the 1970s. One effect was a change in consumer preferences. Some producers were slow to adapt to changing preferences (witness the U.S. auto industry's reluctance to produce small cars), which accentuated the shock on workers and firms when rising energy costs finally forced structural change. Higher energy costs will continue to encourage structural changes as producers become sensitive to their products' operating costs.

The 1960s and 1970s yielded a flood of legislation that began forcing employers to consider traditionally overlooked environmental, health, and safety aspects of production. Most of this new legislation is administered with regulations that limit individual employer flexibility. If employer compliance results in lay-offs or dismissals, can the unemployed workers trace their earnings' losses to governmental actions and demand compensation?

Production planning in the next two decades will be more difficult because of the economic uncertainty induced by export dependence and unprecedented international competition. Since 1960, the share of exports in U.S. gross national product (GNP) almost doubled from 7 to 13 percent. Basic production technologies are now almost universal, making U.S. firms and industries more sensitive to foreign producer and government decisions. Domestic firms that supplied 98 percent of manufactured goods purchased in the United States in 1960 now supply only 93 percent, despite a 40 percent dollar devaluation in the 1970s that made exports cheaper and imports more expensive.[2] U.S. producers see their market shares shrink, and they are unsure of where the pendulum dividing foreign and domestic market shares will stop.

To visualize the employer's planning dilemma in the midst of such uncertainties, it is helpful to separate the demand for a firm's total output into an underlying core demand (predictable a year or so in advance) and an uncertain marginal demand that becomes apparent with relatively little advance notice. Most employers aim to fill both types of demand in order to satisfy consumers and protect their market shares, requiring them to have extra capital and labor on standby status. Profits are increased if this standby capital and labor imposes few costs on employers; machinery that can produce output profitably with an eight-hour work-shift will be even more profitable if a temporary increase in demand justifies the addition of a night work-shift.

Uncertainty, energy costs, and high interest rates have changed preferred capital-labor mixes in this production environment. Employers now want to hire easily shed workers instead of buying machinery that is expensive to finance and operate and which must be paid for whether production occurs or not. Labor is relatively inexpensive and much more flexible, especially when compared to the price of energy and capital.[3] The results of these influences in the 1970s included rapid employment expansion, frequent lay-offs, and declining productivity.

The 1970s employment strategy to cope with uncertainty can succeed only if labor is plentiful and lay-offs are tolerated. But demographic projections indicate that the work force will grow more slowly in the next two decades, just as the clamor for new SSPs indicates that workers are more reluctant to accept lay-offs and dismissals.

Even if we could tap docile new labor supplies (for example, procure alien workers from Mexico) it is not clear that we should. Abundant labor is a two-edged sword. It can hold down wages, increase profits, and spur productivity-enhancing investment, or wage depression can reduce investment incentives enough to discourage investment, slowing the growth in labor productivity. The rate of increase in wages relative to capital-goods costs between 1969 and 1978 was only one-sixth the annual increase between 1948 and 1960.[4] Employer responses are predictable. The capital-labor ratio peaked in 1975 and has been declining as cheap labor is substituted for expensive capital.

Public policies influence employer responses to output-demand uncertainty and company preparations to deal with it. Industrial societies can choose between two basic strategies—encourage standby capital or develop a reserve labor supply. Standby capital can be held within a firm by providing investment tax credits or fast depreciation write-offs that encourage investment even if machinery stands idle, that is, taxpayers can subsidize the costs of employers' standby machinery. At the other extreme a reserve labor supply can be maintained to provide people willing to work part-time or part-year as needed. Either policy gives employers a subsidy to cope with uncertainty.

An intermediate strategy could reduce lay-offs and dismissals by increasing turnover costs, making labor a quasi-fixed cost of production. Public policies can penalize excessive lay-offs by requiring advance notice, severance pay, and employer-paid retraining and relocation assistance. The social safety nets developed in industrial societies increase turnover costs to employers and help to discourage unnecessary lay-offs. Today, industrial economies are reluctant to further increase the cost of firing and dismissal because such policies may discourage the hiring of women, youth, and minorities. Industrial societies walk a tightrope, wanting to provide flexibility for employers but also attempting to ensure full employment and job security for workers.

The trade-off inherent in the reserve-labor option to meet uncertain output demand is flexibility for employers versus job security for individual workers. Industrial societies exhibit a variety of responses to this dilemma. Japan accepts a two-tiered economic structure in which the large companies that employ 30 percent of the labor force protect their workers and pass along uncertainty to smaller subcontractors and their work forces. Japan's largest auto producer, Toyota, gets auto parts from 250 suppliers who in turn rely on 15,000 subcontractors to provide the parts for 70 percent of the cars' value. The Toyota work force is assured job security since the unemployment caused by sales downturns is borne by the subcontractors, "who trim payrolls and thus serve as economic shock absorbers for the industry."[5] As a result, "Toyota never has to make layoffs; but its subcontractors sometimes do."[6] Similarly, Italy provides job protection to workers in some large, mainstream industries but tolerates a parallel sector of subcontractors capable of filling the uncertain component of demand. Economic dualism and subcontracting offer companywide or industrywide job security to these workers producing core demand, and, thus, push flexibility and insecurity into a secondary or subcontracting sector.

Instead of a nonprotected subcontracting or secondary sector, industrial societies can develop flexible work forces to meet demand uncertainties, concentrating the costs of lay-offs and dismissals on particular groups. Housewives, youth, and part-time farmers are classic examples of workers willing to work part of the year as demand conditions warrant. These marginal workers are less concerned with career ladders and job security because they see themselves as primarily housewives, students, or farmers, not as industrial workers. As long as these other alternatives take first priority, marginal workers will be available for insecure jobs.[7]

Alien labor is another source of marginal workers, easy to put on and take off payrolls. Aliens are often a superior work force. They can be trained quickly for many industrial and service jobs. They tend to have high turnover in any case, making it easier to send them home when expected but unpredictable lay-offs are required. Finally, aliens are accustomed to much lower wages and inferior working conditions. The fact that work abroad is seen as a privilege and that migrants are often in a nonresident or uncertain legal status makes them a docile and flexible work force.

Migrant labor permits industrial societies to assure job security for (some) natives and preserves the labor-market flexibility desired by employers. In its strict rotation version, migrants act as micro- and macro-buffers for native workers, who are quickly imported when the need arises and sent home when demand falls. Labor markets are imperfect, however, and industrial societies cannot prevent competition with native workers and some displacement. Moreover, democracies find it difficult to shuttle temporary foreign workers through permanent manufacturing and service jobs and wind up with the problem of integrating a disadvantaged work force.[8]

U.S. manufacturers are now pursuing several strategies simultaneously to cope with uncertainty. Most U.S. employers added easily shed workers throughout the 1970s, helping increase employment by an unprecedented 25 million jobs. But demography may begin to change traditional employment strategies. Hard-hit manufacturers now seem to be "closing problem plants while keeping the rest running on more or less normal schedules"[9] instead of reducing the average work week at all plants to minimize lay-offs.

Most businesses that lay off workers during recessions recall them when demand rebounds. However, most observers believe that some main-line businesses (autos, steel, rubber) will remain smaller than before the last two recessions. "Re-industrializing America will involve closing and not replacing a lot of plants."[10] The result may be more depressed areas with persisting structural unemployment. The decline scenario is familiar. A dominant employer shuts a plant, giving those laid off few alternative job opportunities. The area's income declines, curtailing the service, construction, and trade sectors. Young and mobile workers leave "while older workers with family responsibilities, long personal associations, and owning homes, tend to stay on, exhausting unemployment insurance eligibility and facing little opportunity for re-employment."[11]

The temporary and permanent closure of older and more costly plants in the Northeast and Midwest will accentuate regional economic problems in the 1980s. Multiplant companies use these older plants as shock absorbers for demand fluctuations. The ripple effects of plant lay-offs and closings have their echoes in both the private and public sectors. Laid-off workers spend less, forcing secondary lay-offs and reduced tax revenues. Laid-off workers draw unemployment insurance benefits, and because each state pays the regular UI tax benefits of persons who worked within its borders, the UI system puts the heaviest tax burden on employers in states with "the highest levels and longest durations of unemployment."[12]

Who is most likely to be displaced by impending structural changes? Estimates are necessarily approximate because future demands for labor are not known. Labor force data show that workers in twenty trade-impacted industries—industries that lost jobs between 1964 and 1975—are more likely to be female, minority, and older (table 1-1). These adversely affected workers are more likely to be disadvantaged than the typical manufacturing worker and more likely to have both low earnings and less than average formal education. Thus, aggregate earnings losses in trade-impacted industries are limited initially by low earnings before displacement, but are increased in the long run by worker characteristics that make reemployment more difficult.

Our basic employment issue in the 1980s will be the allocation of increased uncertainty between workers, firms, and government. The initial employer response to uncertainty has been to shift more job-loss risk onto workers, who in turn obtained more inclusive and longer UI protection as well as special protection programs. This shifting of production uncertainty to workers in the form of frequent lay-offs is threatened by the rapidly rising cost of supporting unemployed workers. Furthermore, the work force is aging, which increases the average cost of individual displacements. The high-unemployment youth share of

Table 1-1
The Positive and Negative Impact of Trade on Job Opportunities, 1964–1975

Demographic Characteristics of the Labor Force (Percentage)	Average of the Twenty Industries in Which Trade Had the Most Favorable Impact on Job Opportunities[a]		Overall Manufacturing Average	Average of the Twenty Industries in Which Trade Had the Least Favorable Impact on Job Opportunities
Female	21.5	(23.2)	29.4	41.1
Minority	7.4	(6.0)	10.1	11.5
Under twenty-five years old	15.4	(15.2)	16.4	15.8
Over fifty years old	24.2	(23.8)	26.5	28.0
Family income below the poverty level	5.8	(4.3)	7.0	9.8
Annual earnings under $10,000	72.1	(70.0)	77.4	81.7
Annual earnings under $12,000	83.5	(82.2)	87.2	89.7
High-school education (four years)	39.1	(40.8)	36.6	34.0
College education (four years)	6.9	(7.6)	5.1	3.1
Occupational Breakdowns and Industry Characteristics				
Unionized workers as a percentage of the labor force	40.0	(38.0)	49.0	51.3
Skill measured as a percentage of the average wage in manufacturing (1973)	104.0	(105.2)	100.0	97.8
Skilled workers as a percentage of the labor force	55.8	(59.2)	50.0	38.8
White-collar workers as a percentage of the labor force	36.3	(39.4)	30.3	21.1
Technical intensity (scientists and engineers as a percentage of the labor force)	6.87	(7.76)	3.20	2.29
Technical intensity (R&D as a percentage of sales)	5.90	(6.58)	2.36	1.39
Foreign direct-investment proxy (foreign dividends plus tax credits as a percentage of firm's assets)	.53	(.59)	.34 (Median)	.52

Source: Michael Aho and James Orr, *Demographic and Occupational Characteristics of Workers in Trade-Sensitive Industries* (Washington: ILAB, 1980).

[a]The weighted average in parenthesis is calculated by excluding veneer and plywood; sawmills and planning mills; and logging. These industries should be considered separately due to their relatively high natural-resource content and geographic concentration of production.

the labor force will shirnk, but those unemployed in the 1980s will include proportionally more older displaced workers likely to face severe adjustment difficulties.

Labor Displacement

Shifts in demand and technical changes displace labor in a relatively impersonal manner, since price changes force employers to adjust or go bankrupt. Organizational changes, on the other hand, are far more personal. Company mergers often result in administrative duplication. Most displaced employees above the middle-management level are offered advance notice of dismissal, some form of severance pay, and job-search assistance. Compensation is often provided for influential employees who fear job loss to minimize resistance to a merger or a takeover.

Organizational changes can also displace workers. Companies may close inefficient plants in one community to get a tax loss and open a new plant in another state or abroad, a process displaces blue-collar workers. If the company has been the town's dominant employer, local unemployment rates often double or triple. The earnings losses of displaced workers tend to reduce spending for a variety of local goods and services, causing yet more unemployment and making it harder for the displaced workers to find new jobs. Local governments that have relied on company-paid property taxes must either reduce services or raise sales and property taxes, just when many families in the community are facing substantial income losses.

Workers who are unemployed because of shifts in consumer demands, technological change, and plant closures lose earnings and work-related fringe benefits. Most normal lay-offs end in recall to the old job within one month. Labor displacement is far more costly. Dismissed workers who have few prospects for reemployment with their old employer experience longer periods of unemployment and often take new jobs paying less than their old ones. Because displacement seems to involve more hardship, special assistance programs sometimes supplement normal unemployment assistance for these permanently dismissed workers.

Employed persons who lose their jobs are offered a variety of public and private protections. The most important public protection is federal-state unemployment insurance (UI), which normally pays weekly benefits to qualified unemployed workers for twenty-six weeks. UI is transitional assistance, intended to replace 40 to 60 percent of an unemployed worker's previous net weekly earnings while the worker searches for a job commensurate with work skills and abilities. Regular UI benefits are drawn from the former employer's account with each state's UI fund. When high national or state unemployment rates persist, unemployed workers may be eligible for federally funded extended UI benefits.

Private unemployment insurance agreements supplement public UI payments. The best known is the supplementary unemployment benefit (SUB) system established in the U.S. auto, steel, and rubber industries. Supplemental private UI benefits are available to only a minority of the 20 million U.S. workers belonging to the nation's 176 unions.

Permanently dismissed workers usually draw their first benefits from the public and private UI systems. If dismissal is known to be permanent from the outset and if the workers' union has negotiated a private protection program, then workers displaced by technological changes, plant shutdowns, or company mergers may obtain special assistance for longer periods. Over 42 percent of the collective bargaining contracts that cover 1,000 or more workers require advance notice of dismissal, but only 11 percent require advance notice of technical change (see chapter 3). Some agreements pay adjustment assistance to compensate for loss of seniority and skills. Collective bargaining agreements create private protections that vary enormously in eligibility requirements, amount and duration of benefits, ancillary services provided, and funding and administration.

Government Displacement

The labor displacement of concern here is that traceable to government decisions. New or modified government programs, environmental and health regulations,[13] and changes in international economic policies can directly affect levels of production and employment in impacted industries and firms. Since government works for the common good, a program or policy that generates widespread benefits should not impose undue costs on any worker, firm, or community.[14]

Government actions most likely to prompt special assistance for displaced workers are those where the simultaneous pursuit of incompatible policies is readily apparent. Both full employment and the lower prices from free trade are desired. A tariff concession may lower prices for all consumers but hurt specific workers, firms, and communities. Similarly, the pursuit of a noneconomic goal, such as preserving redwoods for future generations, may displace currently employed loggers. Special protection programs (SPPs) can help displaced workers find new jobs, compensate them for the economic loss of specific work skills, and maintain unemployed workers' incomes during the transition period.

Transportation workers enjoy a plethora of protections. Since 1940 railroad workers have been protected from merger-caused displacement under the act which created the Interstate Commerce Commission. Protection was extended to other transportation workers in the 1960s. The Urban Mass Transportation Act (1964) makes receipt of federal funds for rehabilitation and maintenance of mass-transit systems contingent upon the protection of employed workers for at least six years.[15] The Rail Passenger Service Act (1970) establishing Amtrak similarly requires that employed workers cannot suffer an erosion of wages, benefits, and collective bargaining rights for six years. The Railroad Revitalization

Act (1976) requires railroads seeking federal funds to make agreements protecting workers with relevant unions. The Regional Rail Reorganization Act (1973) guarantees that displaced workers' earnings will remain at previous levels, including any subsequent wages and fringes negotiated by unions. Airline employees are offered job protection by the Airline Deregulation Act of 1978.

Protection for railroad workers is well established because railroad employment has been declining for decades. More recent special protection programs are of greater interest because they could involve far more workers; they provide benefits to both well-organized and unorganized workers; and they provide insight into how an indirect government action may supply the impetus for new SPPs.

The largest SPP illustrates the dilemma of embracing both full employment and free-trade goals. Free trade lowers prices to consumers, but lowering tariffs and removing quotas can displace workers in U.S. factories producing goods that compete with imports. Since tariffs protect U.S. firms and workers from foreign goods, "the government, if it reduces or removes existing tariff protection, is responsible for such injury and should bear at least part of the cost of adjusting to new patterns of trade."[16] To overcome opposition to freer trade, an adjustment assistance program, meant to compensate workers and firms injured by the reduction or elimination of tariffs, was included in the Trade Expansion Act of 1962. Although only 54,000 workers were certified to receive benefits between 1962 and 1975 (and fewer actually got them), the United States became the first country to offer adjustment assistance to domestic firms and workers instead of avoiding tariff concessions or increasing protection against imports because of the threat of domestic dislocations. Adjustment assistance is preferred to maintaining tariffs because it is a one- or two-year social investment that increases efficiency, whereas quotas impose costs on consumers year after year.

The 1965 Automotive Products Trade Act provided up to thirty months assistance to workers displaced by the elimination of duties on auto parts moving between the United States and Canada. Since the United States had exported seven times more auto parts to Canada than it imported prior to the enactment of the act, most of the dislocation was felt in the United States. This three-year SPP was terminated in 1968.

SPPs enacted after 1970 provide benefits to a variety of workers and firms injured by natural or public actions. The Disaster Relief Act (1969) was amended in 1974 to provide regular UI benefits to workers displaced in presidentially declared disasters. The Water Pollution Prevention and Control Act (1972) requires the Environmental Protection Agency (EPA) administrator to hold hearings at the request of workers threatened with displacement due to the enforcement of pollution laws. The Juvenile Justice and Delinquency Prevention Act (1974) requires states requesting federal funds to submit plans detailing arrangements to compensate workers displaced, for example, by a change in drug abuse treatment programs from detention centers to halfway houses. The

Redwood Employee Protection Program (1978) presumes that loggers unemployed between 1977 and 1980 were displaced by park expansion and provides
both weekly payments and ancillary services.

Federal SPPs are proliferating. Caution flags are being raised by those concerned with the diversity of situations that entitle displaced persons to assistance
and the escalating cost of SPPs, especially trade adjustment assistance. But the
concern for proliferation and total costs obscures more specific problems,
including:

1. Lack of worker awareness that SPP benefits are available.
2. Time-consuming determinations of worker eligibility for benefits. Many
   displaced workers are already back at work before they receive any benefits
   because many permanently displaced workers wind up being recalled to
   their old jobs.
3. Inadequate benefits for many workers but such generous benefits for others
   that incentives to change careers or to move out of a depressed area are
   minimal.
4. Ambiguous purposes—are SPPs meant to expedite adjustment to new jobs,
   to compensate displaced workers for industry and/or job-specific losses, or
   to maintain income until another job is found?

Special Protection Programs and Unemployment Insurance

This book examines the growth of publicly funded special protection programs
in the United States. Its thesis is simple: the United States is constructing an
ill-coordinated set of publicly funded categorical protection programs that are
converting the forty-five-year-old UI system into a two-tiered assistance program. Since SPP protections supplement UI benefits, displaced workers have
incentives to trace their displacement to some governmental action and get additional benefits. Since each such displacement traceable to government is unique,
a separate assistance program is created for different groups of displaced workers.
Each program offers a unique set of benefits and sets its own eligibility standards.

The rapid proliferation of SPPs promises to spread protection to enough
jobs so that remaining nonprotected workers will demand coverage. But a master
SPP that covers all jobless workers will be a modified UI system. If the master
SPP covers all workers, some of the benefits now available to a few displaced
workers are likely to be curtailed or eliminated. Workers threatened with such
cutbacks are likely to resist, and to leave policymakers with a difficult grandfather clause versus equity dilemma. Just as the categorical welfare system defies
comprehensive reform, future reorganization and coordination of SPPs with the
UI system will be difficult because it will be hard to devise an equitable and
comprehensive program that both preserves work incentives and is not too costly.

Pressures to begin new SPPs are omnipresent. The original premise of publicly funded special protection programs was that one group of workers should not suffer disproportionately from a government policy undertaken to further the commonweal. A dispersed-benefits but concentrated-costs rationale justified SPPs for displaced Conrail employees, loggers unemployed by expansion of the Redwoods National Park, and airline employees losing their jobs because of deregulation.

Adoption of the idea that changes in public policy hurt some groups who deserve compensation promotes the proliferation of SPPs. The expansion of government economic and regulatory activity means that totally private displacement is becoming a rare event. Should government compensate engineers who moved to Seattle in the early 1970s to design the B-1 bomber rejected by Congress? Who bears the cost of a day-long EPA-ordered plant shutdown in pollution-prone air basins like Los Angeles: the workers themselves, the firm, or the government; or should all three share the costs?

Sensitivity to government action and the foothold provided by current SPPs promise to create pressures for their proliferation. Economics and demography reinforce these pressures. The United States appears headed for a decade of slow growth, especially in areas containing older and less mobile workers. Research shows that older workers in declining areas suffer most from involuntary lay-off or severance. The U.S. economy, relatively insulated from the ever-changing world economy in the past, is now more subject to internationally transmitted shocks than ever before. The ability to find some government culpability for displacement, the dim prospects for quick reemployment in many areas, an aging labor force, and the fact that legislators are supportive of measures to protect their constituencies all promise new demands for special protection programs.

Several reform options are explored here. The first basic policy question is whether individuals, firms, and/or communities should be compensated for involuntary job losses traceable to government actions. The search for economic efficiency suggests that most assistance be directed toward individuals since they typically have the fewest resources to cope with change and they are usually better prepared to make drastic changes, particularly in location, than are firms or communities. Unlike firms, individuals cannot store their main asset, time; nor can they diversify and work simultaneously in several industries to reduce displacement risks.

Special protection programs offer compensation for the training, skills, and seniority acquired and lost because of a publicly inspired change. UI, on the other hand, partially replaces the temporarily lost wages of experienced workers. Conceptually, SPPs compensate for a one-time loss of income while UI partially replaces temporarily lost earnings. Theoretically, the two losses should be handled separately. In practice, however, no one knows how to calculate the exact economic losses involved in career and geographic changes until a displaced worker is back at work, preventing lump-sum benefit payments at the time of dismissal. Because it is impossible to calculate total losses at the time displacement occurs, most SPPs pay easily terminated weekly benefits just like UI.

Most SPPs pay benefits from general tax revenues, a reflection of the general nature of the expected benefits from the government decisions that cause labor displacement. As SPPs proliferate, spending on SPPs is becoming a significant share of UI payments. If UI and SPP programs are kept separate, SPP programs could wind up paying more total benefits than does UI.

Demands for new SPPs also depend on employer responses to structural change. All signs point to an accelerated pace of structural change. Current economic incentives encourage employers to hire easily shed workers instead of buying fixed-cost capital, thus increasing temporary and permanent lay-offs.

Summary

Labor-displacing change is an inevitable part of a dynamic economy. Displaced workers are eligible for different kinds of assistance. Most laid-off workers are eligible for twenty-six weeks of unemployment insurance benefits that replace 40 to 60 percent of previous weekly earnings. Some laid-off workers covered by supplemental unemployment benefits agreements receive additional compensation. Mass dismissals are sometimes regulated by specially negotiated private protection programs that compensate displaced workers for loss of seniority and job-specific skills.

Government pursuit of conflicting goals (for example, moves toward free trade and full employment) prompted the creation of special protection programs. These federal programs mitigate the losses of workers, firms, and communities adversely affected by a government policy meant to generate widespread benefits. The sixteen SPPs added $3 billion to the nation's $20 billion unemployment insurance outlay in FY 1981.

The proliferation of categorical special protection programs for the deserving displaced threatens to convert the nation's basic UI system into a two-tiered assistance program. The inequities and inefficiencies of separate certification, benefit, and delivery systems make the call for consolidation into a single UI system inevitable. If reforms are not accomplished soon, it may be impossible to grandfather current SPP recipients into a comprehensive UI system.

Employers have responded to 1970s production uncertainties in ways that increase lay-offs and reinforce demands for new special protection programs. Unprecedented labor force growth held down real wages while the interest and energy costs of buying labor-saving machinery skyrocketed. The result was a substitution of labor for capital and a transfer of the costs of production uncertainties to workers, since employers hired easily shed workers instead of buying fixed-cost capital. Reforming the UI system to eliminate the need for SPPs also requires reforms to discourage unnecessary lay-offs and dismissals.

Notes

1. These labor shifts may not displace labor if new labor force entrants move directly into the expanding sector, for example, the factory worker's son into services.

2. "The Reindustrialization of America," *Business Week,* June 30, 1980, pp. 58–59.

3. Total Jobs Keep Rising Despite Many Layoffs and Talk of Recession," *Wall Street Journal,* March 24, 2980, p. 1.

4. "Investment and the Growth in Productivity," *Morgan Guaranty Bank Survey,* September 1979, p. 11.

5. L. Kraar, "Japan's Automakers Shift Strategies," *Fortune,* August 11, 1980, p. 109.

6. *Wall Street Journal,* March 3, 1980 p. 1. The story notes that this sub-contracting system "has become one of the Japanese automakerr' greatest competitive strengths," helping to explain their reluctance to build U.S. assembly plants and buy U.S. components.

7. Michael Piore, *Birds of Passage* (New York: Cambridge University Press, 1979).

8. Philip Martin, *Guestworker Programs: Lessons From Europe.* (Washington: Department of Labor, 1980).

9. "Unemployment: The Worst is Yet to Come," *Fortune,* January 26, 1981, p. 10.

10. Ralph Winter, "Many Companies See Chancy Times Ahead and Act to Cut Danger," *Wall Street Journal,* March 23, 1981, p. 1.

11. *The Structure of Unemployment in Areas of Substantial Labor Surplus* (Washington: Joint Economic Committee, 1960), p. 1.

12. Charles Killingsworth, "Employment Policy for Recessions" in *An Employment Policy to Fight Recession and Inflation* (Washington: National Council on Employment Policy, 1980), p. 28.

13. Regulatory changes can make machinery obsolete prematurely. But the investments needed to conform to new regulations can also displace labor, since most new machinery will save labor. The estimated $58 billion investment required by auto companies to meet fuel efficiency standards has been labeled very worthwhile for auto producers because it will also eliminate 128,000 jobs. *The Economist,* June 10, 1978, p. 91.

14. Richard Freeman makes the same point by noting that "private as well as public "insurance" or redistribution schemes are needed to make sure that those injured by economic changes (which benefit society as a whole) do not bear an enormous cost." "Comment" in *The Impact of International Trade and Investment on Employment* (Washington: DOL, ILAB, 1978) p. 100.

15. In mid–1982, the Reagan administration proposed a new mass-transit grant program that would cancel most current labor protections. This may be a harbinger of an attempt to eliminate traditional transportation SPPs.

16. The President's Message Transmitting the Administration's Trade Bill, H.R. Doc. No. 314, 87th Congress, 2nd Session (1962), p. 11.

2 Costs of Displacement

Unemployed persons can be divided into three groups. Except during recession, about 40 percent of the unemployed are persons looking for their first job or reentering the labor force after several months or years. The second group consists of persons temporarily laid-off for several weeks or months and persons who quit their last job or were fired. The final group are the displaced—persons dismissed by employers for nondisciplinary reasons who do not expect to be recalled to their old jobs. Separating the temporarily laidoff from the permanently displaced is difficult because some temporary lay-offs become permanent dismissals and some permanent dismissals wind up being only temporary lay-offs.

Permanent dismissals usually mean earnings losses for workers, sometimes reflect a firm's losses, and occasionally signal the demise of an entire community. The circumstances of worker dislocation vary greatly, as does the distribution of losses between workers, firms, and communities. The labor displacement envisioned by policymakers when creating SPPs involves the permanent dismissal of a relatively large number of workers at once or within a brief period. However, there may be less of this kind of labor displacement than is commonly believed.

Labor displacements have several common features. Since a group of workers is involved, displaced workers are likely to include older workers normally protected from lay-offs by seniority. Many of these older workers have developed work skills that are most useful to their former employer. Most have no recent job-search experience. The psychological blow of dismissal and the fact that older workers may be unfamiliar with local labor markets often lengthens their period of unemployment.

Some displacement occurs in communities where a single firm dominates employment. A plant closure in such situations typically reduces employment in secondary or supplier establishments and makes it difficult for displaced workers to get new jobs. Displaced workers, especially older persons who own houses and have other local investments, may be reluctant to move to areas with jobs.

Two general approaches are used to explore the costs of labor displacement. One can begin with macro-data, isolate that fraction of unemployment due to lay-offs, and trace the reemployment experience of laid-off workers. Alternatively, an aggregate picture can be obtained by generalizing from a series of firm or industry studies of displacement and reemployment. The best cost-of-displacement evidence comes from expensive longitudinal studies that track a displaced worker for several years after he has found a new job to see how fast his earnings rise and whether he experiences lay-offs frequently in his new job.

There are remarkably few studies of the link between unemployment and economic hardship. Orley Ashenfelter is reported to have said that this lack of research stems from offsetting fears: "trade union leaders are afraid that a new study would find relatively little hardship, and conservatives and businessmen fear that a study might show an extremely high incidence of hardship."[1] Available evidence indicates that both sides may be correct for particular groups of unemployed workers. For most workers, a short period of unemployment is not a severe financial hardship. These laid-off workers can usually receive UI, sometimes supplemental unemployment insurance benefits, and in some instances the earnings and fringe benefit protections of a currently employed spouse. However, for some workers, especially older workers laid-off by plant shutdowns and workers just entering the work force without work experience or eligibility for UI, unemployment can result in severe economic hardship.

Total Unemployment

Monthly household data provide estimates of the unemployment rate, the average number of unemployed persons, and the average duration of unemployment (table 2–1). The simplest macro-estimate of the cost of unemployment is made by multiplying the average weekly wage times the average number of weeks of unemployment. In 1980, average weekly earnings were $235. During a typical week in 1980, an average 7.4 million workers were jobless. The composition of the unemployed labor pool changes from week to week, but one estimate of the earnings losses due to unemployment is $92 billion (7.4 million x 235 x 52 weeks). This gross figure is of limited use for policymakers. It overstates total income losses because the unemployed generally had been earning lower than average wages and because public and pirvate transfers partially replace lost earnings.

The March Current Population household survey provides data on work experience during the previous year. Most workers are employed all year with one employer. Most unemployed workers experience only one brief spell of unemployment in any year, but a significant number of workers have several jobless spells. The surprise is the high incidence of unemployment. In 1980, one in five workers experienced some unemployment and in 1982, 30 million persons will experience unemployment.

Economic hardship usually increases the longer a person remains unemployed. Figure 2–1 shows that most laid-off workers find a job within five weeks, that is, over 40 percent of those unemployed in a given month were not unemployed in the previous month.[2] However, during recession periods like 1975–1976– or 1981–1982, the unemployed are almost evenly divided between those

Table 2-1
Selected Unemployment Statistics, 1960–1981

Year	Household Data[a] Unemployment				Unemployment Insurance Statistics[c]	
	Rate (in Percent)	Average Monthly Number (in 000s)	Average Duration (in Weeks)	Total Unemployment (in 000s[b])	Number of First Payments (in 000s)	Average Cumulative Duration (in Weeks)
	(1)	(2)	(3)	(4)	(5)	(6)
1960	5.5	3852	12.8	14151	6754	12.7
1961	6.7	4714	15.6	15096	7067	14.7
1962	5.5	3911	14.7	15256	6073	13.1
1963	5.7	4070	14.0	14211	6041	13.3
1964	5.2	3786	13.3	14052	5498	13.0
1965	4.5	3366	11.8	12334	4813	12.0
1966	3.8	2875	10.4	11387	4139	11.2
1967	3.6	2975	8.8	11564	4619	11.4
1968	3.6	2817	8.4	11332	4197	11.6
1969	3.5	2832	7.9	11744	4212	11.4
1970	4.9	4088	8.7	14565	6397	12.3
1971	5.9	4993	11.3	15851	6627	14.4
1972	5.6	4840	12.0	15287	5780	14.0
1973	4.9	4304	10.0	14498	5328	13.4
1974	5.6	5076	9.7	18318	7715	12.7
1975	8.5	7830	14.1	21104	11160	15.7
1976	7.7	7288	15.8	20447	8560	14.9
1977	7.0	6855	14.3	19512	7985	14.2
1978	6.0	6047	11.9	–	7569	13.3
1979	5.8	5963	10.8	–	8075	13.1
1980	7.1	7448	11.9	–	9992	14.9
1981	7.6	8080	13.9	–	–	–

[a]Bureau of Labor Statistics, *Employment and Earnings.*

[b]U.S. Dept. of Labor, *Work Experience of the Population,* Special Labor Force Reports. Total unemployed includes all persons experiencing unemployment at some time during the calendar year: data from 1960–1966 includes unemployed fourteen years and older. 1967–1978 includes sixteen years and older.

[c]Employment and Training Administration, *Handbook of Unemployment Insurance Financial Data,* 1938–1976 and *The Employment and Training Report of the President: 1981,* Table F-13.

out of work less than five weeks, five to fourteen weeks, and fifteen weeks and over (in June 1982, 33 percent, 32 percent, and 34 percent, respectively). The average duration of unemployment climbs also, to sixteen weeks in 1976 and seventeen weeks in 1982.

These data indicate that most unemployed persons suffer relatively short spells of unemployment. However, the longer people are unemployed, the higher the probability that they will remain unemployed for a long time. Individuals unemployed for more than two months are likely to remain unemployed six

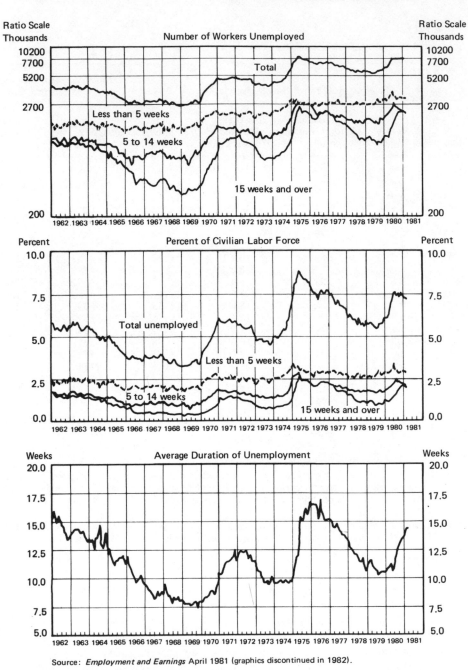

Figure 2-1. Duration of Unemployment, 1962–1981 (seasonally adjusted)

months or more. One-third of the unemployed surveyed in June 1982 had been looking for a job less than five weeks. However, another 1.8 million workers— 17 percent of the unemployed—had been without work for twenty-seven weeks or more.

Duration of unemployment estimates must be interpreted carefully. George Akerlof believes that average duration data severely underestimate the length of time many unemployed workers are without a job.[3] Akerlof argues that workers between jobs who are unemployed less than four weeks account for 60 percent of all bouts of unemployment during the year, but this favored group is only 5 percent of all unemployed persons at any point in time. Lumping these short-term unemployed with workers who suffer repeated spells of unemployment and workers with one long period of unemployment obscures the fact that the average duration of unemployment for the long-term unemployed is eight months or more. Estimates from 1974 indicate similarly that most workers suffer only brief spells of unemployment, but that one-half of all unemployment was due to bouts of unemployment lasting three months or more.[4] If these distribution analyses are correct, then most long-duration unemployment is due to a relatively few persons with prolonged periods of joblessness.

The difference between single bouts of unemployment and repeated and prolonged joblessness can be illustrated by comparing demographic groups. In 1979, unemployed women were jobless an average 9.6 weeks, compared to 12.0 weeks for men. But women had so many more bouts of joblessness that their unemployment rate was one-third higher than the male unemployment rate. Similarly, teenagers were jobless an average of only 7.0 weeks, versus 12.0 weeks for older workers, but teenagers were jobless so many more times in 1979 that their unemployment rate was three times that of older workers.

The first defense against economic hardship for permanently and temporarily dismissed workers is unemployment insurance. UI payments are available to only about one-half the unemployed. In 1977, almost eight million unemployed workers received a first UI payment (that is, they were employed in 1976). To these first time recipients we must add the unknown number of carryover UI recipients—perhaps two million persons who began to get UI checks in 1976 and continued getting them in 1977. This group of about 10 million insured and unemployed workers averaged two seven-week spells of unemployment to receive an average fourteen weeks of UI benefits.[5]

The 1981–1982 recession appears to be causing more economic hardship than any other postwar downturn. The Department of Labor estimates in mid-1982 that in eight major industrial states 36,000 laid-off workers exhaust their UI benefits every week. In May 1982, less than 40 percent of the 10.3 million unemployed (compared to two-thirds of the unemployed in the 1975 recession) were eligible for UI benefits, possibly reflecting the fact that many workers laid off in 1980 were not reemployed long enough to qualify for UI benefits when unemployment struck again. Unemployed auto and steel workers accustomed to

UI and company-paid supplemental unemployment benefits (SUB) are getting reduced SUB payments or no SUB benefits at all. Over 40 percent of the steel industry's 250,000 hourly workers are laid off, and half of these unemployed workers may be replaced by automated equipment in a smaller steel industry. The 1981–1982 recession has not yet run its course, but current indications are that it signals a degree of economic hardship that most unemployed workers were able to avoid in the past four decades.

This study is concerned with persons unemployed because they have been dismissed from their last job with little prospect of recall. However, permanently dismissed workers cannot be isolated from other job losers who have been laid off. *Lay-offs* are defined as "suspensions without pay lasting or expected to last more than seven consecutive calendar days, initiated by the employer without prejudice to the worker." Unemployment statistics do not include information on how long the lay-off is expected to last. Even if they did, expectations may be misleading because lay-off intentions change.

Monthly household data group the unemployed into four categories. Job losers include persons permanently dismissed, workers on temporary lay-off, and workers who are fired.[6] Job leavers voluntarily quit their old jobs. Reentrants are seeking another job after being out of the work force and new entrants never held a full-time job before.

Each group is identified separately in monthly statistics. In June 1982, for example, 60 percent of the 10.4 million unemployed were job losers. Another 8 percent were job leavers. Almost 22 percent of the unemployed were reentrants and 10 percent were new entrants.

Only 20 percent of the job losers were on temporary lay-off. In fact, persons on temporary lay-off are a small fraction of all the unemployed (table 2–2), between 10 and 20 percent of all unemployed persons since 1975. Since many teens have never held a full-time job from which they can be laid off, only 9 percent of the unemployed teens were on temporary lay-off in December 1981.

Table 2–2
Temporary Lay-offs, 1975–1981

Year	Total Both Sexes	16–19 Years Old Both Sexes	20 and Older	
			Male	Female
	(1)	(2)	(3)	(4)
1975	21.2	7.6	28.8	20.5
1976	14.3	5.7	20.3	12.7
1977	12.4	4.7	17.9	11.6
1978	11.5	4.1	17.2	11.1
1979	14.0	5.4	20.7	13.1
1980	19.8	6.2	28.4	17.4

Source: Bureau of Labor Statistics, *Employment & Earnings,* Household data, Table 13, January editions 1977–1982.

Permanently dismissed workers are included with the 40 percent of the un-employed who lost their jobs and are not on lay-off. But these 4.2 million unem-ployed workers include persons fired and those dismissed and not expecting to be recalled. If we can assume that the fraction of those who are fired does not change over time, then table 2-3 shows that the number of permanently dis-placed workers has remained at about one-third of all unemployed persons since 1975. Once again, prime-aged males are most likely to be in this other job loser category—between 43 and 50 percent of all adult males who are unemployed lost their last jobs and are not on temporary lay-off. Involuntary dismissals are twice as frequent as temporary lay-offs for adult women and three times more common for teens.

Job leavers voluntarily quit one job to take or seek another. Quits usually rise when unemployment is low (figure 2-2) and it is easy to find another job (1966-1968) and fall when unemployment and lay-offs rise (1974-1975). Most studies conclude that quits have declined since 1960, in part because quitting without good cause can disqualify a worker from receiving UI benefits.

Turnover data show how firms hire and dismiss workers. Accessions include new hires and workers recalled from lay-offs. Separations are quits and lay-offs. How many laid-off workers are recalled to their old jobs? Table 2-4 indicates that two-thirds of all workers laid off from manufacturing firms got recalled in 1980. However, the two-thirds recall ratio is a sharp drop from the average 80 percent recall ratio that prevailed from 1960 through 1975.[7] Preliminary 1982 data suggests an even sharper drop, reflecting the severity of the 1981-1982 recession. Moreover, manufacturing turnover data paints too optimistic a picture. Even within manufacturing, the larger firms dominating the lay-off sample offer more stable employment.[8]

The total losses of temporarily laid-off workers are obtained by summing their net losses while unemployed and earnings losses or gains after reemploy-ment. Most manufacturing lay-offs are relatively short (under two months) and

Table 2-3
Other Job Losers, 1975-1981

Year	Total Both Sexes	16-19 Years Old Both Sexes	20 and Older	
			Male	Female
1975	34.2	18.0	46.2	29.5
1976	35.5	16.9	49.8	30.8
1977	32.8	14.5	47.3	29.1
1978	30.0	14.9	44.4	26.1
1979	28.8	15.1	42.8	24.2
1980	32.1	17.1	43.2	27.5
1981	34.2	16.6	46.2	30.1

Source: Bureau of Labor Statistics, *Employment & Earnings,* Household Data, Table 13, January editions 1977-1982.

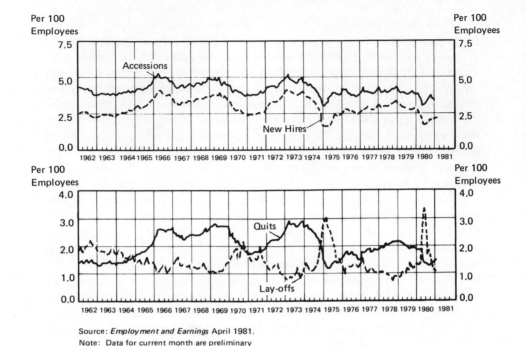

Source: *Employment and Earnings* April 1981.
Note: Data for current month are preliminary

Figure 2–2. Labor Turnover Rates in Manufacturing, 1962–1981
(seasonally adjusted)

Table 2–4
Manufacturing Turnover Rates, 1975–1981

	Turnover Rates per One-Hundred Employees		
Year	Recalls (in percent)	Lay-offs (in percent)	Ratio of Recalls to Lay-offs
	(5)	(6)	(7)
1975	N.A.	2.1	N.A.
1976	1.0	1.3	0.77
1977	0.9	1.1	0.82
1978	0.7	0.9	0.78
1979	0.7	1.1	0.64
1980	1.1	1.7	0.65
1981[a]	0.8	2.2	0.36

Source: Bureau of Labor Statistics, *Employment & Earnings,* Establishment Data, Table D–3, January 1982.
[a]October 1981 data.

most workers who are recalled to their old jobs earn their old wages or more.[9] Most laid-off manufacturing workers have at least 50 percent of their wages replaced by UI and supplemental insurance benefits; some retain medical insurance benefits while on lay-off or are covered by another household member's insurance.[10]

However, if laid-off workers must find new jobs, they are often required to accept wage cuts.[11] Older workers generally fare worst in the search for new jobs, largely because they have seniority and skills specific to their old employer that impede horizontal job shifts.[12]

Permanent Displacement

If most lay-offs are only a temporary earnings blemish, involuntary displacement is more likely to leave a permanent scar. Studies of workers displaced by plant closings in the early 1970s support the conclusion that people permanently displaced, unlike temporary lay-offs, suffer substantial losses in earnings for prolonged periods of time.[13] These earnings losses are larger if the firm had been paying high wages and if many of the displaced workers are older. Costly displacements include those that result from the closing of steel mills, rubber plants, and auto operations.

Two basic kinds of displaced worker studies are available. The most common are before-and-after studies that compare earnings before displacement and at several times afterward. These studies isolate displaced workers and generally underestimate true earnings losses because the before-and-after comparison does not take into account generally rising wages. Longitudinal studies, on the other hand, compare the earnings paths of displaced workers with either a control group of employed workers or with workers on temporary lay-off. The longitudinal studies generally find larger and more persistent earnings losses after displacement.

Before-and-after studies of earnings losses from plant closings include interviews with workers after enough time has elapsed to observe labor market behavior, usually six months to three years. Most studies of permanent displacement find that terminated workers' new jobs pay less than their old ones. Haber's summary of seventeen plant-closing studies between 1929 and 1961 found that most displaced workers took new jobs that paid less than their old jobs even though general wage increases which occurred in the interval between jobs should have allowed them to move into higher paying jobs. Three of the studies found that after five years the median income of a displaced worker was only half his predisplacement income. A 1964 Bureau of Labor Statistics survey of plant-closing studies came to similar conclusions.[14]

Is the initial earnings drop after reemployment temporary or permanent? Even though few longitudinal studies track displaced workers after they find their first new job, most researchers assume that initial earnings losses signal continued wage depression for displaced workers. Although interviews after reemployment are not conclusive, they support the idea that earnings will continue to be lower. The reason is simple: "The forty-year-old worker with fifteen years of seniority who starts anew in the job market competes on less favorable terms than he did when he found his former job. Now he must compete with individuals who are relatively younger and better educated than he."[15]

Reemployment at lower wages is only part of a displaced worker's problem. Most displaced workers are unemployed or underemployed for several months before they find another job. For example, in the seventeen studies reviewed by Haber only 37 percent of the displaced workers found new jobs within one month and many of these new jobs were only temporary. Neuman's study of 916 displaced workers found that fully 41 percent remained unemployed after two years. This study also found that displaced women averaged four months more unemployment than displaced men.

Control group longitudinal studies compare earnings losses to expected earnings if there had been no displacement. Expected earnings are based on human capital theory, which argues that earnings should rise over time as cumulative seniority and experience make a worker more valuable to his employer (figure 2-3). A displaced worker suffers a drop in earnings (year 0) and then slowly creeps back up to his old wage (a) or exceeds it (b). Total losses are represented by the shaded area. Note that a before-and-after study would show an earnings gain for worker b after four years even though he had experienced earnings losses.

The Center for Naval Analyses has done most of the longitudinal earnings loss studies to date. These studies conclude that earnings losses are substantial. Further, these losses increase if the displaced workers are prime-aged males; employment was previously stable (little turnover and attrition); and the industry pays high wages. Earnings losses after displacement is unionized basic industries—autos, steel, meatpacking, rubber, aerospace, and refining—often exceed 25 percent over a six year period (a worker displaced in 1970 earns $10,000 less between 1970 and 1976 than he would have earned if he had not been displaced).[16]

Earnings loss data have been admirably summarized in a recent International Labor Affairs Bureau (ILAB) report (table 2-5). Data from the closing of forty-one plants in 1969, 1970, or 1971 show that earnings losses are substantial in the first two years after displacement and that high wage, unionized workers suffer most. Workers in low-wage industries (for example, shoes, cotton weaving, men's clothing) are more likely to find new jobs that pay wages comparable to the previous job. Displaced workers who find new jobs are vulnerable to new lay-offs, since they lack the seniority to avoid dismissal during recession.

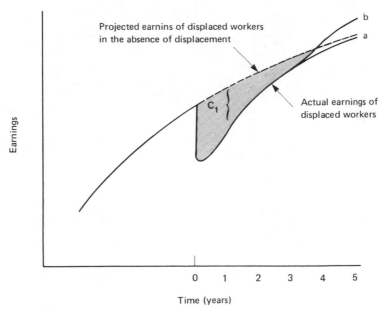

Projected earnins of displaced workers
in the absence of displacement

C_1

Actual earnings of
displaced workers

b

a

Earnings

0   1   2   3   4   5

Time (years)

Figure 2–3. Earnings Losses Caused by Displacement

A recent Mathematics study of 1,500 involuntarily displaced workers found minimal displacement losses.[17] The Mathematics study examined the experience of workers eligible for trade adjustment assistance (TAA) benefits in 1976. TAA was established to assist workers permanently displaced because of imports. However, Mathematics found that most TAA recipients were not permanently displaced. Interviewed three and one-half years after being laid off, most displaced workers rightfully had expected their lay-offs to be temporary. Four-fifths of the 900 displaced workers who received their first TAA payment in 1976 expected to be recalled to their old jobs, and 72 percent actually were. A control group of laid-off workers that received only UI payments was less hopeful of being recalled and few workers actually were. Surprisingly, almost two-thirds of the 1,500 displaced workers were able to keep their health insurance while unemployed either because a collective bargaining agreement required continued coverage or because they were covered by an employed spouse's health plan.

The reason TAA recipients fared so well in the Mathematics study is that most (77 percent) were not permanently dismissed. The majority of TAA recipients (60 percent) wound up on temporary lay-off. These workers, mostly in steel and autos, never really severed connections with their old employers. Supplemental unemployment benefits and maintenance of health insurance allowed private benefits to augment federal TAA and make these lay-offs relatively painless.

Table 2-5
Earnings Losses of Prime-Aged Male Workers

Industry	First Two Years	Subsequent Four Years	Average Annual Percentage Loss					
			First Two Years	Subsequent Four Years	1972 First Year	1972 Second Year	1974 Third Year	1975 Fourth Year
	(1)	(2)	(3)	(4)	(5)	(6)	(7)	(8)
Automobiles	43.4	15.8	24.1	14.6	20.21	10.7	3.05	11.68
Steel	46.6	12.6						
Meat-packing	23.9	18.1						
Aerospace	23.6	14.8						
Petroleum refining	12.4	12.5	15.9	16.4	19.36	17.16	12.78	11.24
Women's clothes	13.3	2.1						
Electronic components	8.3	4.1	10.1	.2	2.85	-4.75	-8.85	-1.82
Shoes	11.3	1.5			.85	-8.93	-14.46	-12.05
Toys	16.1	-2.7						
Television receivers	0.7	-7.2						
Cotton weaving	7.4	-11.4	7.6	5.2	5.84	1.44	-3.29	-2.69
Flat glass			16.3	16.2	35.21	28.82	21.17	21.18
Men's clothing			21.3	8.7	6.4	-3.12	-12.30	-18.38
Rubber footwear			32.2	-.9				

Source: International Labor Affairs Bureau (ILAB), U.S. Department of Labor (Washington: ILAB, July 1979).

Most of the other 17 percent of those explicitly in temporary lay-off status were women on short-hours in the apparel industry. TAA, but not UI, allows workers to collect benefits and to work a reduced number of hours each week, once again mitigating earnings losses.

One-fourth of the 900 TAA recipients were permanently displaced. These workers' characteristics reinforce the mental image of displaced workers and confirm the results of other studies. Many were older, drawn from low-wage declining indusrries like apparel and foortwear, and likely to remain unemployed for extended periods. Permanently displaced workers remaining in the labor force averaged an initial jobless spell of forty-two weeks and were likely to be unemployed more frequently than regular UI recipients during the three and one-half year study period.

Compared to a control group of permanently dismissed workers eligible only for regular UI benefits in 1976, permanently displaced workers getting a first TAA payment in 1976 had a higher incidence of earnings losses (75 versus 65 percent). This loss is greater for permanently displaced TAA recipients— $50 weekly versus $30 for regular UI recipients. Permanently dismissed workers do suffer real earnings losses. These losses are more severe in at least one area with a special job protection program—import-sensitive industries.

The 1981–1982 recession appears to be inflicting more lasting losses on displaced workers. Surveys indicate that up to half the workers displaced by plant closings remain jobless for a year or more. Unionized auto and steel workers who lose jobs that pay $10 or $12 hourly wages must often accept new jobs paying $5 to $6 hourly, a labor-market reality that encourages many older displaced workers to accept early retirement. The 1981–1982 recession is a painful reminder that downward economic mobility accompanies long downturns.

Mobility and Earnings Losses

Displacement is a permanent earnings scar for many workers, especially older persons in high-wage unionized industries. But how are earnings losses affected by mobility? Can a displaced worker reduce seemingly inevitable earnings losses by moving to another city?

Most studies indicate that mobility pays off. Displaced workers have three basic choices: immediately look for another job in the same labor market; retrain for another job close to home; or move to another area and work for the same or another employer. The fact that transfers and mobility seem to increase earnings (or at least reduce losses) has important implications for adjustment assistance and regional programs. The recent debate engendered by the Agenda for the Eighties 1981 recommendation that declining northeastern and midwestern cities should be allowed to continue declining, and the uproar over the concept that cities are not permanent, underscores the political resistance to any kind of large-scale mobility induced by despair.

Stern's study of 838 workers displaced by Armour's closing of meat-packing plants in Kansas City in 1964 divided affected workers into mobile, retrained, and new local groups.[18] Only 12 percent of the displaced workers elected to transfer to other Armour plants, but these workers had 1967 earnings 21 percent higher than in 1963, the last full year before plant closing. Most (71 percent) of the displaced workers looked for another job in the Kansas City area. Even though unemployment averaged only 4.5 percent in Kansas City and most wages increased over the four year period, this new local job group had earnings 14 percent lower in 1967 than in 1963.

One unexpected finding of the Stern study was that workers who retrained before looking for another Kansas City job had lower earnings after four years than displaced workers who immediately plunged into the local labor markets. Retrained workers averaged $6,000 in 1963. Four years later, they earned only $4,300. Stern suggests that the apparent failure of training may be due to self-selectivity, that is, the best workers don't need training to find another job. Even though the retrained workers were not statistically different from the others, the suspicion lingers that unmeasurable "appearance, aggressiveness, and motivation" differences between the groups may account for the ineffectiveness of training.[19]

The Stern study probably overestimates the payoff to mobility because most Armour transfers moved from one higher-than-average wage meat-packing job to another. A pilot project promoting the interstate movement of unemployed workers through the employment service shows that free long-distance telephone service, $500 job-search grants, and up to $1,500 relocation reimbursements did get 1,749 unemployed workers to move at an average cost of $1,085.[20] However, two-thirds of the workers initially recruited for the Job Search and Relocation Assistance program dropped out when they learned that they were expected to move out of state. The employment service screened potential movers by asking them if they were willing to relocate and only telling persons answering affirmatively about the program. In general, unemployed persons younger than thirty-four, blacks, men, and persons with less education were willing to move.[21] Even though relocation may prove the most efficient way to regain lost earnings levels, unemployed workers seem to require a battery of incentives and services to consider moving. Even then, most do not move.

Propsects for increased mobility are dimmed by demography and the fact that housing costs are rising fastest in areas with jobs. Older workers are reluctant to move because they are more likely to have made local investments that tie them to an area and because they and their children are reluctant to leave friends and relatives.[22] The doubling of mortgage interest rates between 1975 and 1981 makes older workers displaced from jobs in the Northeast and Midwest especially reluctant to sell their slowly appreciating homes covered by low fixed-interest mortgages to buy considerably more expensive homes at unprecedented high and variable mortgage rates.

The 1980–1982 auto recession that encouraged some unemployed Michigan workers to seek jobs in Texas illustrates these impediments to migration. The laid-off auto workers earned $10 to $12 hourly in Michigan, but the service jobs available in Texas often paid only $4 or $5 hourly. Older workers and the unskilled had problems finding steady jobs and affordable housing, especially when forced to sell their Michigan homes at a loss. Unemployed workers continue to move to the South and the West, but at a slower rate. In addition, anecdotal evidence suggests that some frustrated movers are returning to their old homes.[23] Relocation may be optimal, but demographics and economics do not promise to expedite it.

Reemployment Functions

Displaced workers suffer earnings losses because they are unemployed and then often reemployed at lower wages than before. We know that three interdependent factors influence reemployment: individual characteristics; the industry of last employment; and local labor market conditions. Mobility and adjustment assistance are partially dependent on all three factors.

The interdependence of all three influences makes isolation of the relative importance of each very difficult. For example, if auto assembly was the industry of last employment the displaced worker is likely to be a prime-aged male in a high unemployment northeastern or midwestern city. Unemployed auto workers have union-negotiated private benefits to supplement both regular and special state and federal assistance.

Accurate predictions of the total costs of job loss require far more information than is currently available. However, labor-force projections indicate that males aged forty-five and older will drop from 26 to 23 percent of the male work force by 1995.[24] Females forty-five and older are projected to stay at 17 percent of the female work force. However, prime-aged women workers (twenty-five to fifty-four) will jump from 25 to 34 percent of the total work force. The minority share of the total work force will increase—blacks alone will become 14 percent of the work force by 1995. Hispanics may outnumber blacks by then, comprising another 15 percent of the work force. Since older, female, and minority workers are most likely to suffer from job loss, we can expect increasing losses from and resistance to dismissals.

Policymakers, especially trade negotiators, are aware of wage losses and demographics. Insufficient and ineffective assistance programs often complicate tariff negotiations, Multilateral trade negotiators in 1979 were aware of the work-force composition of sensitive industries that would be affected by concessions. Workers in these sensitive industries tend to be female, older, with a higher percentage of minorities, to have fewer skills and lower earnings (table 2–6). To protect such workers, "tariff cuts were not made in many highly import-sensitive

Table 2–6
Characteristics of Workers in the Industries Given Special
Consideration during the Multilateral Trade Negotiations

	Sensitive Industries	Manufacturing Average
Female	62.3	28.6
Minority (nonwhite)	11.3	9.9
Under twenty-five years of age	17.2	16.4
Over fifty years of age	29.6	19.8
Family income below the poverty level	7.4	4.2
Annual earnings under $10,000	92.0	77.9
High school (four years)	29.9	36.6
College (four years)	2.8	5.1
Skill measured as a percentage of the average wage in manufacturing (1973)	71.8	100.0
Unskilled workers	71.5	49.8
Blue-collar workers	82.7	69.6

Source: *Trade and Employment Effects of Tariff Reductions Agreed to in the MTN,* International Labor Affairs Bureau (ILAB), U.S. Department of Labor (Washington: ILAB, 1979).

sectors."[25] This avoidance strategy will be harder to maintain as the U.S. work force changes and more economic sectors become vulnerable to international competition.

Summary

Displaced workers not expecting to be recalled to their old jobs are a significant fraction of the unemployed. Most laid-off workers are recalled to their old jobs within two months. But the 10 to 20 percent of laid-off persons not recalled usually suffer prolonged unemployment and often wind up in new jobs that pay lower wages than did their old jobs.

The workers suffering most from displacement are older, experienced workers in high-wage, unionized industries that are shrinking their work forces: for example, autos, steel, and rubber. Many of these workers began their careers with the firm from which they were separated. Permanent dismissal makes their firm-specific seniority rights and job skills worthless.

Displaced workers also suffer from the loss of dignity that accompanies a steady job. Although conclusive evidence is sparse, it is often asserted that displacement leads to a helplessness that promotes drinking and marital instability.

Relocation sometimes reduces the earnings losses associated with displacement. But relatively few displaced workers relocate or retrain for a new job.

Relocation incentives must be especially generous for older workers with local friends and relatives who have low-interest mortgages on their slowly appreciating homes. Theory and observation suggest that relocation efforts should focus on younger displaced persons.

Notes

1. *New York Times,* June 15, 1980, p. 1.

2. Thomas Bradshaw, "Employment in Perspective: A Cyclical Analysis of Gross Flows in the Labor Force" (Washington: U.S. Department of Labor, Bureau of Labor Statistics, 1977), Report 508, p. 1.

3. Summarized in *Business Week,* March 30, 1981, p. 16.

4. Kim Clark and Lawrence Summers, "Labor Market Dynamics and Unemployment: A Reconsideration," *Brookings Papers on Economic Activity,* 1(1979):13-72.

5. Based on a sample of 15,000 insured persons in Arizona and Pennsylvania. K. Classen, "Unemployment Insurance, The Duration of Unemployment, and Post Employment Earnings" (Ph. D. Diss. UCLA, 1978).

6. Unpublished Bureau of Labor Statistics data indicate that 0.4 percent of the manufacturing work force is discharged for cause each month, or 4.8 percent per year. If the manufacturing discharge rate is applied to the entire work force, it appears that four million workers are discharged each year for excessive absenteeism, fighting, horse play, insubordination, theft, disloyalty, and incompetence. Very little is known about the unemployment experience of these workers because most are not eligible for UI benefits.

7. See for example, Martin Feldstein, "The Importance of Temporary Layoffs; an Empirical Analysis," *Brookings Papers on Economic Activity,* 3, 1975.

8. Indeed, an examination of 1974 hiring and separation rates found that the typical firm hires as many new persons each year as it employs, on average, during the year (construction and retail trade employers hire more new persons than their average employment). See Malcolm Cohen and Arthur Schwartz, "U.S. Labor Turnover: Analysis of a New Measure," *Monthly Labor Review,* October 1980, p. 11 (table 1).

9. Classen, Unemployment Insurance.

10. A survey of 2,585 employers in late 1978 to early 1979 found that 60 percent of all firms in the private nonfarm sector offer group health plans to some or all of their employees. These group health plans cover 90 percent of all private nonfarm employees. However, only 7 percent of the firms allow laid-off employees to continue coverage by self-payment of premiums (one-third of the construction firms permit self-payment for continued coverage). Department of Labor News Release 81-194, April 20, 1981.

11. George Borjas, "Job Mobility and Earnings over the Life Cycle," *Industrial and Labor Relations Review,* April 1981, pp. 365-376.

12. George Borjas and S. Rosen, "Income Prospects and Job Mobility of Younger Men," (based on the Parnes data) mimeographed (Ohio State University, 1979).

13. Harry Gilman, "The Economic Costs of Worker Dislocation: An Overview," mimeographed (Washington: ILAB; July 13, 1979), p. 9.

14. Haber, L. Ferman, and J. Hudson, *The Impacts of Technological Change* (Kalamazoo, Mich.: Upjohn Institute, 1963) and *Case Studies of Displaced Workers* (Washington: Bureau of Labor Statistics Bulletin 14, 1964), Another valuable Upjohn study, published after this manuscript was completed, generally confirms the findings of earlier displacement studies but notes that today's studies are far more concerned with community reactions and that emphasis has shifted from the impact of unemployment on the individual to the impact on the family. Jeanne P. Gordus, Paul Jarley, and Louis Ferman, *Plant Closings and Economic Dislocation* (Kalamazoo, Mich.: Upjohn Institute, 1981).

15. J. Stern, "Consequences of Plant Closure," *Journal of Human Resources,* 7:19.

16. Lewis Jacobson, "Earnings Losses of Workers Displaced from Manufacturing Industries," (Alexandria, Va.: Center for Naval Analysis Working Paper 169, 1976.

17. Corson et al., *Survey of Trade Adjustment Assistance Recipients* (Final Report, Mathematical Policy Research Princeton, New Jersey, December 1979).

18. J. Stern, "Consequences of Plant Closure," p. 17. The group percentages are calculated from Table A-4.

19. Ibid., p. 16.

20. *Wall Street Journal,* January 20, 1981, p. 1.

21. Charles Mueuer, "Migration of the Unemployed," *Monthly Labor Review,* April 1981, pp. 62-64.

22. H. Parnes et al. *From the Middle of the Later Years* (Draft report, Ohio State University, May 1979), pp. 3-28.

23. Carol Hymowitz, "Some Migrants to Sun Belt Retrun," *Wall Street Journal,* November 16, 1981, p. 25.

24. Drawn from the Bureau of Labor Statistics middle labor-force growth projections. See Howard Fullerton, "The 1995 Labor Force: A First Look," *Monthly Labor Review,* December 1980, pp. 11-21.

25. "Executive Summary" in *Trade and Employment Effects of Tariff Reductions Agreed to in the MTN* (Washington: Department of Labor, June 15, 1979).

3 Job Protections

Most U.S. workers can be dismissed at their employer's whim, or, in the words of the Supreme Court, "employers may dismiss their employees. . . . for good cause, for no cause, or even for causes morally wrong."[1] Few employers capriciously dismiss employees, since a fair and equitable personnel system is usually necessary to attract and keep good workers. The most general lay-off protection available to workers is a tight labor market that forces employers to hoard labor, to weigh current wage costs against the need to search for and train new workers if business rebounds. Unemployment insurance helps keep trained but temporarily redundant workers available to their former employers.

Displacement or permanent dismissal is not constrained by the same market forces because employers foresee no immediate need to rehire discharged workers. No general protection from such displacement is available; a worker has no inherently compensable property right in his current job that requires an employer to pay for the right to dismiss workers. This general lack of displacement protection means that "it is still both simple and cheap for companies to sack workers and close factories in the United States."[2] Nonetheless, some employers provide early (two weeks) notice of dismissal, facilitate transfers to other establishments of the same company, or extend fringe benefits for a short period after dismissal. These largely voluntary employer actions assist some workers but do not create job property rights.

Three general types of laws influence dismissals—torts, civil rights, and labor relations laws—but none automatically creates a job property right. Tort law allows workers injured by the negligence of an employer or dismissed because of third-party interference to sue for money damages. Tort laws rarely affect the employment relationship today because most workers now turn to workers' compensation programs for assistance if they are injured at work.

Civil rights laws regulate the hiring and dismissal procedures employers must follow. No law requires that any specific individual be hired or dismissed. Civil rights legislation simply says that employers may not make hiring or dismissal decisions contingent on race, color, national origin, religion, sex, age, veteran status, physical handicap or, in some localities, sexual preference. Civil rights laws allow employees discriminated against in hiring or discharged in violation of law to collect monetary damages from the date of an employer's illegal action. Similarly, workers complaining of health, safety, or environmental violations may not be downgraded or discharged in retribution for filing a complaint.

Labor relations laws create the same type of indirect job property rights—an employee's illegal dismissal for union activity may allow the discharged worker to collect back pay from the date of the employer's unlawful action. But labor relations laws go further. They allow employers and unions to negotiate agreements regulating dismissals. Job property rights can be created in labor-management agreements that provide compensation for job loss. In addition, an agreement may specify when and how employees slated for dismissed are to be selected, what kinds of attrition procedures must be followed before anyone can be discharged, and the extent of ancillary services available to discharged workers, including maintenance of fringe benefits, retraining and job placement assistance, and seniority rights to transfer to other plants.

About 20 percent of the nation's 106 million workers belong to labor unions that negotiate agreements regulating wages and working conditions. Labor-management agreements regulating labor displacement cover all types of involuntary discharge (plant closures, company mergers, and technological changes), simply the replacement of men with machines, or more general automation programs that make major changes in normal production practices. Few agreements prohibit labor-displacing change. Most agreements only require employers to inform unions about the timing and rate of displacing change. Labor laws require bargaining over the effects of labor-displacing changes but do not clearly define employer obligations to bargain over the labor-displacing change itself.[3]

Unlike European workers, U.S. workers have no general property rights in their jobs that require compensation for discharge. Civil rights laws permit redress for unlawful employer dismissals and labor relations laws allow the creation of compensable rights, but most (nonunionized) workers are governed by the traditional master-servant principle of employment at will. Since both employers and workers can sever the employment relationship at will, compensable job property rights are not part of Anglo-Saxon common law. Some labor lawyers argue that an employer's ability to terminate a nonunion employee at will violates the constitutional guarantee of due process.[4]

Several state courts have begun to restrict a private employer's right to discharge nonunion workers. At least 60 million nongovernment, nonunion workers can be dismissed by employers who do not have to justify their decisions. Jack Stieber estimates "that companies in private industry discharge one million permanent employees each year without a 'fair hearing'."[5] California courts have held that workers fired capriciously can sue for lost wages and punitive damages. Under this fairness doctrine, a worker discharged in violation of promises and procedures set forth in an employee handbook or for refusing to obey an employer's order to break the law may recover damages from his former employer.

Some state courts take an employee's length of service into account when deciding if a dismissal is justified. A California appeals court ruled that American Air lines must justify the dismissal of a nonunion employee with eighteen years service. State courts are beginning to argue that nonunion employees are entitled to fair dealing and just cause before discharge. These state court decisions seem to imply "a kind of tenured status that prohibits dismissal without just cause."[6] The result may be more careful worker evaluations and better documentation of reasons for discharge.

It is not clear how far this drive to protect nonunion workers will go. The Connecticut legislature refused to enact a 1975 proposal that would have prohibited the dismissal of any employee with at least five years service unless the employer could demonstrate "just cause or a bona fide business reason for reduction in the work force." Similar legislation is pending before the Michigan and New Jersey legislatures. The proposed 1980 Corporate Democracy Act would have amended the National Labor Relations Act to make an employer guilty of an unfair labor practice if employees were dismissed without just cause.

Most business executives negotiate severance pay on an individual basis. A 1981 survey found that 80 percent of the fired executives interviewed got an average three months severance pay and many retained their fringe benefits for several months. The same report notes that companies are beginning to provide at least job-hunting help to dismissed secretaries and clerks.[7]

Nonunion white-collar employees are sometimes awarded severance pay and relocation assistance. Basic manufacturing companies with unionized blue-collar work forces usually fire white-collar employees without compensation, but nonunion technology companies often give cash bonuses to workers slated for dismissal. Xerox, for example, offered up to fifteen weeks pay to induce quits among the 2,380 workers it planned to dismiss in 1982. Polaroid expected 1,000 workers to voluntarily take advantage of a lump-sum severance plan that pays one month's salary for each year worked to older employees. White-collar lay-off plans vary considerably, but the 1981 recession made many more white-collar workers aware of job insecurity.

This chapter examines the evolution of general job loss protections. The first section outlines the protections available to all persons in our social welfare system, and the second reviews the unemployment insurance system that pays benefits to temporarily and permanently dismissed workers. The third section analyzes negotiated displacement protections.

The Income Security System

The overall performance of the economy determines national income, the size of the economic pie. The income security system redistributes part of the national income. Four distinct types of programs comprise the nation's income security system. *Income support* or public assistance programs (such as Aid to Families with Dependent Children (AFDC)) provide cash assistance to low-income persons in order to raise their incomes to a satisfactory level. *Earnings replacement* programs help maintain previous income levels when earnings cease for predictable (retirement) or unpredictable reasons (unemployment, disability). *Essential service* programs are intended to assure everyone access to minimum levels of food, medical care, and housing. Finally, *preventive* programs make some education compulsory, facilitate training and retraining, and establish minimum levels of public health.

Preventive programs are financed from general tax revenues and cover all persons in the United States. Most preventive programs are financed by income and property taxes that are assumed to generate revenues on the basis of ability-to-pay. Many preventive programs have added income-conditioned components, such as free school lunches for the children of low-income parents and public service employment (PSE) and training options for disadvantaged workers.

Earnings-replacement programs are usually work-conditioned, making eligibility for benefits contingent on past employer and worker contributions. Payroll taxes are collected to finance earnings replacement benefits in case of temporary unemployment, disability, retirement, and death. The major earnings replacement programs—social security, workers compensation, and unemployment insurance—provide benefits that are considered earned entitlements. The major provisions of earnings-replacement programs are summarized in table 3-1.

Income support and essential service programs are the welfare components of the U.S. income security system. Regardless of one's work history, eligibility for benefits depends on current income and assets. These welfare programs include public assistance (AFDC) and supplemental security income (SSI) as well as food stamps, housing assistance, and medical care programs. Although these welfare programs accounted for only 20 percent of the $286 billion in federal transfer payments to individuals in FY 1980, they include the most controversial parts of the nation's income security system (table 3-2).

Expenditures for income maintenance have increased rapidly. Between 1960 and 1980 broadly defined social welfare outlays increased from 25 to 50 percent of the federal budget. To curb expenditure growth rates, more and more income-security programs are means-tested, in an attempt to confine program benefits to the truly needy.

The single most important income maintenance program available to a displaced worker makes benefits contingent on his work history. Unemployment insurance replaced an average 38 percent of an unemployed worker's previous weekly pay for an average fifteen weeks in 1980. UI benefits can be supplemented with food stamps, available to all persons with income below the poverty line established for their place of residence and family status ($7,500 for an urban family of four in 1980). If unemployment persists, the unemployed person's family may be entitled to AFDC payments that also entitle the family to Medicaid and sometimes priority for Public Service Employment (PSE) or retraining. The normal earnings replacement scenario for a displaced worker includes UI and perhaps food stamps. These first-line defenses may be followed

Table 3-1
Earnings Replacement Programs in the United States, 1976

Reasons for Earnings Loss	Earnings Replacement Source	Jurisdiction
Temporary unemployment	Unemployment insurance	State, federal
	Public service employment	State, federal
Disability resulting from work only total and partial	Workmen's compensation	State
	Veterans compensation	Federal
	Black lung program	Federal
Other	Sick leave	Public and private employees
Short-term	Temporary disability insurance	State, private
Long-term	Social security (disability) insurance)	Federal
	Long-term disability insurance	Private
	Early retirement pensions	Most public and private pensions
Retirement and death low-to-middle income classes	Social security (old age and survivors insurance)	Federal
Middle-to-upper income classes	Social security (old age and survivors insurance)	Federal
	Pensions	Most employers
	Annuities, life insurance, and other savings	Private

Source: Adapted from *Setting National Priorities* (The Brookings Institution, 1976), p. 511.

by a widening safety net of cash assistance, other essential services, and labor-market assistance if joblessness persists.

Displaced older workers can take early retirement and receive social security benefits after UI payments are exhausted. The same cash assistance and essential service benefits are available. Few older workers undergo retraining. Most find programs for the elderly more generous then the benefits of assistance programs available to all low-income persons.

Unemployment Insurance

Temporary and permanent lay-offs mean individual workers have no earnings until a new job is found. Unemployment insurance partially replaces lost earnings for unemployed persons meeting the eligibility rules set by each state. UI payments are drawn from a state fund that collects payroll taxes from employers.

Table 3-2
Outlays for Benefits to Individuals, Fiscal Year 1980

Program	Outlays (millions of dollars)	Percent of All Outlays	Means-Tested
Retirement and Disability			
Armed forces	12,127	2.09	No
Federal civilian	14,739	2.56	No
Railroad	4,737	0.82	No
Miners	1,840	0.32	No
Veterans	11,689	2.02	Partially
Social Security	116,573	20.13	No
Subtotal	161,705	27.93	
Health			
Medicare	35,025	6.05	No
Medicaid	13,957	2.41	Yes
Federal civilian retirees	631	0.11	No
Veterans' hospital & medical	6,276	1.08	Partially
All other	2,694	0.47	Partially
Subtotal	58,583	10.12	
Education			
College student aid	3,683	0.64	Yes
Guaranteed loan interest subsidy	1,408	0.24	No
Social Security student benefits	1,976	0.34	No
Veterans' education benefits	2,342	0.40	No
Subtotal	9,409	1.63	
Unemployment Compensation	18,004	3.11	No
Public Assistance			
Subsidized housing	5,377	0.93	Yes
Nutrition programs	4,802	0.83	Mostly
Food stamps	9,117	1.57	Yes
SSI for aged, blind, and disabled	6,411	1.11	Yes
AFDC and other welfare	7,308	1.26	Yes
Earned income tax credit	1,275	0.22	Yes
Low-income energy assistance	1,564	0.27	Yes
Refugees	368	0.06	Yes
Subtotal	36,222	6.26	
Miscellaneous	1,155	0.20	—
Grand Total	285,078	49.24	—

Source: *Reducing the Federal Budget: Strategies and Examples, FY 1982-1986,* A Congressional Budget Office Study (Washington: United States Government Printing Office, February 1981).

The employer-paid payroll tax is designed to discourage temporary lay-offs, hence the threat of higher UI taxes does not stop plant closures or permanent dismissals. The model UI recipient is an experienced worker laid off because of cyclical or seasonal business downturn who remains willing and able to return to his old job or to take a comparable job elsewhere.

The unemployment insurance system is administered by the states under federal guidelines. The 1935 Social Security Act's Title III (amended by the Federal Unemployment Tax Act) permits the federal government to levy a payroll tax on most employers—now 3.4 percent of the first $6,000 each employee earns ($204 for most workers). Employers get credit for 2.7 percent ($162) of the required federal payment if they instead pay the 2.7 percent tax into an approved state UI system that actually pays benefits to unemployed persons. The remaining 0.7 percent tax is paid to the federal government and is used to administer both the federal and state systems and finance the extended benefit program and a federal UI loan fund.

If a state does not have an approved UI system, the entire 3.4 percent payroll tax would be collected by the federal government and the state would have to find other monies to pay UI benefits. Not surprisingly, all fifty states, the District of Columbia, Puerto Rico, and the Virgin Islands have established approved UI systems. Each state, however, has its own rules to determine UI eligiblity and benefit levels.

All employers pay a uniform 0.7 percent federal tax to administer the UI system, but the additional state tax that pays actual UI benefits depends on each employer's experience rating. Experience ratings reflect employer lay-off records. Firms with frequent lay-offs pay higher UI taxes. The experience rating system and the size of each state's UI reserve fund determine the actual payroll tax. When unemployment is low and UI reserves are adequate, the actual UI tax may be near zero. In normal times, tax rates typically fall in the 2.7 percent range.[8] During severe recessions, when many laid-off workers are drawing UI benefits, employer tax rates may be 4 to 6 percent of each employee's first $6,000 in earnings.

Despite UI tax rates based on experience ratings, most UI tax systems use some of the taxes paid by stable employers to subsidize firms with unstable employment. For example, a utility with few lay-offs may face a UI tax rate of only 1.5 percent but still pay three times more in UI taxes than its laid-off workers collect in benefits from the utility's UI account. A garment manufacturer may be assessed a 5 percent UI tax and still contribute only one-fifth of the total benefits that its laid-off employees collect.

Amendments in 1978 extended UI coverage to almost all wage and salary jobs (separate UI programs cover federal employees, railroad workers, and persons leaving the armed forces).[9] Over 97 percent of all wage and salary jobs (versus 60 percent in 1950) are now covered by UI, which paid $20.1 billion to 10.1 million persons in FY 1981. Two prominent exclusions are most of the domestic workers employed in private homes and many casual farmworkers.[10] Individual states can and do provide UI coverage for these workers, but federal law does not mandate their inclusion to keep a state's UI system approved.

UI benefits are not automatic; an individual must apply for them. Although each state establishes its own eligibility standards, minimum-earnings and length-of-employment tests generally determine whether an unemployed person will actually receive UI payments. All states require a worker to have earned a minimum amount of money in the base period, usually $700 to $1,500 during the previous year or the first four of the previous five quarters. Many states require that earnings be received in at least two quarters and require at least fourteen to twenty weeks of work during the previous year. A few states simply establish a minimum earnings requirement and say nothing about previous employment (for example, California requires applicants to have earned at least $20 weekly for eight weeks and a total of $900 during the previous twelve months or to have earned $1,200 during the previous twelve months if the $20 weekly for eight weeks requirement is not met).

UI benefits are only available to laid-off persons satisfying eligibility criteria. In nonrecession times, fewer than one-half the unemployed receive UI benefits. Most unemployed persons do not qualify for UI benefits because they have not worked before (new entrants) or recently (reentrants); or because they were separated from their last job under disqualifying conditions (fired from their last job or voluntarily quitting previous jobs); or because they have exhausted their UI benefits. Most persons unemployed because of a labor dispute are not eligible for UI benefits.

No state offers UI benefits to new workers or those reentering the work force after an absence of a year or more.[11] The unemployed worker without previous employment may need UI benefits most, but the notion that UI is an earned benefit makes it hard to extend eligibility to unemployed persons without work experience under the current benefit system.

UI benefits are only available to unemployed persons with recent earnings and employment experience who continue to search for a new job. Availability for work requires that UI recipients register at a public employment office and usually obliges unemployed workers to search for work independently of the employment service's job matching efforts. An unemployed worker receiving benefits is disqualified if he refuses a "suitable job."

The fact that millions draw UI while the newspapers carry pages of help wanted ads is more an opinion about the desirability of individual flexibility than an inherent problem of the UI system. The vacant job may be in another state or require a long and expensive commute. More often, the job is not suitable in terms of recent work experience. In such circumstances, is an unemployed person refusing suitable work? UI claimants usually have an employment record with the previous employer. Should that work history be ignored and the worker forced to take a job with unstable employers who have high rates of worker turnover or else lose benefits? Finally, should unemployed workers be forced to choose between a lower-paying job outside their normal occupation or industry and a benefit cutoff? Secretary of Labor Donovan argued that unemployed workers should be forced to accept written work offers from any employer who pays at least the minimum wage or a wage equivalent to a worker's weekly UI benefit after thirteen weeks of UI payments. He believes that such a rule would reduce UI payments by $285 million annually.[12]

The duration of UI benefits became an early target of Reagan administration budget cutters. Unemployed workers are eligible for an additional thirteen weeks extended UI benefits after their normal twenty-six weeks of benefits run out if the national unemployment rate for the 87 million UI-insured workers exceeds 4.5 percent for at least thirteen weeks and a state's unemployment rate exceeds the level that automatically triggers eligibility for extended benefits. In 1980, two million people received $1.8 billion in extended benefits, a cost shared by the states and the federal government. To slow the rapidly rising costs of extended benefits, Labor Secretary Donovan proposed the elimination of the national UI trigger and higher state triggers to save $1.2 billion in FY 1982. In addition, UI benefits are to be limited to unemployed individuals who were employed at least twenty weeks in a fifty-two week base period. Adoption of these reforms and lower unemployment are projected (table 3-3) to decrease UI outlays by $2 billion by FY 1982.[13]

Local UI claims administrators decide whether an individual applicant for UI is entitled to benefits. Workers may appeal benefit denials and employers can appeal a decision to pay UI benefits to a previous employee before a UI referee. This administrative decision may be appealed to a board of review and later appealed to the courts.

UI benefits aim to replace at least one-half an unemployed worker's lost earnings for six months. The actual UI systems of the various states, however, wind up replacing one-third to two-thirds of an unemployed worker's lost earnings. Maximum weekly benefits (table 3-4) range from $84 (Puerto Rico) to $196 (District of Columbia). The average 1981 weekly benefit is expected to be $101, about 42 percent of the average weekly wage of UI-covered workers. States exhibit no consistent pattern in maximum weekly benefits, but industrialized states and states with strong unions tend to pay most. It is often argued that UI benefit variability results in horizontal inequities—unemployed workers in similar circumstances get benefits contingent on an accident of geography.

Table 3–3
Estimated Unemployment Insurance Benefits, 1981–1982

	Total Benefits (in millions)	Recipients (in millions)	Average Weekly Benefit
Fiscal year 1980	$13.8	$10.0	$ 99
Fiscal year 1981	$20.1	$10.1	$101
Fiscal year 1982	$18.1	$ 9.6	$107

Source: Department of Labor News Release, March 13, 1981, p. 14.

Table 3–4

Maximum Weekly Unemployment Insurance Benefits for a Single Person, 1981

Highest		Lowest	
District of Columbia	$196	Puerto Rico	$ 84
West Virginia	184	Alabama, Georgia, Mississippi	90
Pennsylvania	175	Arizona	95
Wisconsin	166	Maine	104
Louisiana	164	Missouri, Florida	105
Minnesota	162	Nebraska	106
Hawaii	157	Tennessee	110
Oklahoma	156		
Colorado	154		
Delaware, Utah, Alaska	150		

Source: U.S. Department of Labor, 1981.

Why do some states pay such low UI benefits? "Competition among the states to retain or attract industry by minimizing the tax burden on employers"[14] is said to explain the tendency to pay low UI benefits in some states. States paying low UI benefits sometimes attract unstable and mobile industries whose high labor turnover make UI taxes a significant part of the business's costs.

Benefits are usually available to eligible workers after a one-week waiting period, although eleven states have no waiting period and ten states retroactively pay this first week's benefits. Most states stop UI benefits after twenty-six weeks (nine states continue payments for thirty-nine weeks), but eligibility for twenty-six weeks of UI benefits depends on an individual's length of employment and earnings. Since 1970, the federal government requires states to extend UI benefits if the national and a state's unemployment rate exceed a trigger level. Extended UI benefits may not exceed thirteen weeks, but temporary federal supplemental benefits allowed some unemployed workers to collect benefits for sixty-five weeks in 1975–1977. Because many UI recipients live with families that have another wage earner, UI benefits are taxable if family income exceeds $25,000 or if an individual's total income exceeds $20,000.

The UI system temporarily replaces the lost earnings of most laid-off workers. In recent years the UI system has been under attack for paying too much for too long and discouraging unemployed workers from accepting new jobs. Several empirical studies have attempted to isolate how much unemployment is traceable to increased UI benefits. A 1968 increase in the ratio of UI benefits to average wages, for example, found that the overall unemployment rate in Pennsylvania and Arizona was raised nearly one-half of a percentage point (0.4 percent). Researchers finding significant work disincentives stress the fact that UI benefits are tax-free for most recipients; thus, UI payments replace a greater percentage of previous net earnings than the average 42 percent of gross earnings.[15]

Higher UI payments and longer eligibility periods are alleged to increase the duration of unemployment. Stephen Marston found that the average UI recipient was likely to be unemployed 16 to 31 percent longer than his uninsured counterpart. This longer duration unemployment arises from more selective job search and the fact that UI recipients must remain in the labor force looking for work to continue receiving benefits. Another study argues that the duration of unemployment is increased by almost eight weeks for persons drawing UI benefits compared to unemployed persons not eligible for or not bothering to apply for benefits.[16] Such conclusions must be interpreted very carefully, however, since the unemployed drawing UI benefits are probably different (older males with more job experience) than noneligible, inexperienced teens and women.

The work disincentive effects of UI are very hard to measure. Most studies are based on economic conditions in the early 1970s, a period characterized by increases in UI benefits alongside rising unemployment rates. Studies confined to periods of increasing benefits and generally falling unemployment rates may come to different conclusions. Most studies assume a constant (linear) relationship between benefit increases and longer periods of unemployment. However, it is more likely that the relationship is nonlinear; successive increases in UI benefits may lead to accelerating unemployment durations. Finally, even if higher benefits lead to longer periods of unemployment, society may benefit if reemployed workers are better satisfied with their new jobs and thus more willing to stay with their new employer.

The UI system has been confronted with two issues—"avoidance of work disincentives on the one hand and provisions of adequate support on the other"—from its inception.[17] Critics who stress UI's work disincentives imagine a job search procedure that has workers gradually reducing the wage they want and employers increasing the wage offered. Unemployed workers, especially those dismissed after being with one employer for many years, are slow to reduce their reservation wages to realistic levels. If better labor-market information were available, the match could be made sooner and the duration of unemployment cut. Better information and counseling could separate the unemployed into those who really want to work and others, presumably saving some UI benefits, since benefits are denied most frequently to applicants who are considered unable or unavailable for work.[18]

This mechanical view of the labor market's matching efficiency ignores wage dispersion and a psychological reality. The changing occupational structure in the United States has increased inequality in hourly earnings, a trend accentuated by greater relative wage increases for higher wage occupations.[19] A displaced worker without recent job-search experience should be expected to search longer for a new job because of increased wage dispersion alone. Affluence and psychology reinforce this tendency to search longer. An affluent society should not expect unemployed workers to immediately reduce their wage expectations. It is hard to explain to a discharged worker that his value of marginal product is suddenly reduced 20, 30, or 40 percent. Affluence and income security should be expected to lengthen the average duration of unemployment.

The extended benefits available in the mid-1970s prompted a debate on the insurance-income maintenance trade-off in the income security system. Most observers view the UI system as a social insurance program that pays benefits to eligible workers who earned them. However, successive benefit extensions increased UI costs and prompted arguments that UI was also an income maintenance system that should restrict extended benefits to unemployed workers who really needed them. The policy issue is not resolved, but reductions in extended benefits will maintain the distinction between UI as an insurance program and UI as an income maintenance system.

Special job protection programs imitate the UI system. Each federal program has a legislated origin, a financing mechanism (a special tax or general revenue), standards for benefit eligibility, procedures to appeal administrative decisions, and criteria for determining the amount and duration of benefits. The same issues of job search, suitable alternative work, work disincentives, and benefit variability from program to program arise, but are usually settled by liberal interpretations favoring workers—interpretations often required by law. No employer rating system pits worker against employer because benefits are often paid from general revenues. Indeed, SPPs often provide benefits to both employers and workers.

The UI system is the oldest, largest, and most comprehensive system providing payments to temporarily and permanently displaced workers. The UI system has been supplemented by private protection agreements. These private protection plans can be divided into supplemental unemployment benefit (SUB) plans to augment UI benefits during an expected temporary lay-off and programs mitigating permanent job losses.

Private Displacement Protections

Most private protections for job loss are contained in labor-management agreements. The most common U.S. union policy toward technological changes (machines replacing men) is still passive acceptance.[20] However, union attitudes toward job security are changing because of a wave of total or partial plant closures and relocations and labor-displacing company mergers. Job security is the bargaining issue in 1982.

Union members acquire property rights in the way they do their jobs through tradition or through written work rules. Many labor-displacing technical changes require alterations of these work rules; for example, the rule that every plane had to have a nonpilot flight engineer until the 1960s, the rule that cargo had to be repacked by West Coast longshoreman on the docks before it could be loaded onto ships until 1969, or the rule that train crews had to include a redundant fireman (dropped in 1972). In each instance, employers had to buy out a way of doing work before they could introduce an efficiency-increasing change.

Although many workers believe that management should compensate them whenever it wants to change their jobs, few U.S. workers enjoy such protection. Written job protections in the private sector are confined to unionized workers and management personnel at or above middle ranks. This section outlines the most common negotiated job protection arrangements.

Lay-offs are either temporary or permanent. It is often difficult to predict whether an announced lay-off will be temporary or permanent because changing economic conditions or company circumstances can convert planned temporary into permanent lay-offs or vice versa. Most collective bargaining agreements do not distinguish temporary and permanent lay-offs. Instead, agreements specify job protections that may change with the duration of a lay-off.

Planned temporary lay-offs due to seasonal or cyclical demand downturns are minimized by reducing work hours and proscribing overtime. Supplemental unemployment benefits are sometimes available to those actually laid off. Laid-off workers protect their seniority rights if they remain available for recall.

Permanent displacements stem from technological changes and partial or total plant closures that displace labor. Technological change is usually the easiest displacement to deal with because unions can bargain over its consequences and some (most) workers may be retrained to operate the labor-displacing machines. Technological changes that displace a large number of workers sometimes prompt special agreements requiring advance notice of lay-offs, transfer and retraining rights, and severance pay.

Displacements caused by plant closures create more problems. The general movement of jobs southward and westward means that closure leaves few local job alternatives in the Snowbelt states, where many recent plant closures have occurred. The fact that other businesses and entire communities are affected by the closure of a major plant means that workers facing displacement want to bargain privately and publicly over the terms of the shutdown. The main bargaining issues are whether the plant really must be closed (usually an employer's unilateral decision); the advance notice that must be given to workers; the amount, form, and duration of any severance pay or retraining assistance; and the extent of relocation and transfer benefits.

Displacement protections fall into three overlapping categories. *Job protections* are an attempt to minimize lay-offs by keeping workers in their jobs. *Adjustment assistance* minimizes earnings losses for laid-off workers. *Special agreements* are usually ad hoc responses to large-scale lay-offs and dismissals.

Many contract provisions simultaneously provide job protections, adjustment assistance, and special agreement aid. Advance notice, for example, can expedite planning for transfers and can permit spread-the-work work sharing. Advance notice can also allow the accumulation of funds to compensate workers ultimately displaced. The following list contains the most common job security clauses found in 1,537 labor-management agreements covering 7 million workers surveyed by the Bureau of Labor Statistics in 1978.[21] Table 3-5 summarizes the frequency and coverage of each provision.

Table 3-5
Frequency and Coverage of Job Security Clauses

	Clause	Percent of Agreements	Workers Covered	Percent
Advance notice				
Lay-off	669	43.5	3,346,100	47.8
Permanent displacement	160	10.4	710,800	10.2
Technical change	171	11.1	1,221,350	17.4
Extended vacations	72	4.7	463,900	6.6
Transfer rights	456	29.7	3,297,100	17.4
Relocation allowances	201	13.1	1,989,800	6.6
Management restrictions				
Subcontracting				
Limited	862	56.1	4,691,500	67.0
Prohibited	8	0.5	71,250	1.0
Not limited	01	0.7	20,950	0.3
Regulation of overtime	51	3.3	441,150	6.3
Limiting crew size	339	22.1	1,520,050	21.7
Restriction of work by				
nonbargaining unit				
personnel	969	63.0	4,608,050	65.8
Slack work provisions				
Reduced work hours	275	17.9	1,922,950	27.5
Work sharing	112	7.3	614,950	8.8
Wage guarantees				
Weekly	141	9.2	834,050	11.9
Monthly	2	0.1	10,000	1.4
Greater than one month				
but less than one year	36	2.3	356,950	5.1
Annual	9	5.9	91,600	1.3
Retention of seniority rights				
during lay-offs	1,096	71.3	5,215,750	74.5
Preferential rehire	175	11.4	1,905,150	27.2
Retraining				
Apprenticeship	667	43.5	3,176,850	45.4
On-the-job	574	37.3	354,250	5.1
Tuition aid	81	5.3	861,250	12.3
Severance pay	500	32.5	2,640,700	37.7
SUB	220	14.3	1,947,400	27.8

Source: *Characteristics of Major Collective Bargaining Agreements* (Washington: BLS, Bulletin 2065, 1980).
Note: Based on 1,570 agreements covering 7.0 million workers in 1978.

Attrition

Normal or accelerated attrition reduces the size of the work force without involuntary displacement. The company freezes hiring and waits for retirements, transfers, deaths, and discharges to reduce the work force gradually. Incentives to encourage early retirement and speed up attrition are often offered.

Advance Notice

Advance notice of lay-offs allows workers time for job search and permits unions to negotiate displacement assistance. Advance notice ranges from twenty-four hours to two years. Some contracts contain advance notice clauses instead of severance pay. Most advance notice requirements are short, normally less than one month. Management often argues that a longer notice of permanent dismissal reduces productivity (the best workers leave first), increases absenteeism, and hurts worker morale. Unions want more advance notice to consider job-saving concessions and/or to facilitate job search. The United Rubber Workers-Firestone contract, for example, required Firestone to keep its Akron facility operating until April 1981 even though the company wanted to close it in March 1980.[22] Legislation pending in several states would require companies to announce plant closures one to two years in advance.

Almost two-thirds of all collective bargaining agreements contain requirements to give advance notice of lay-offs, plant shutdowns, relocations, and/or technological change. Of the agreements containing advance notice clauses in 1980, two-thirds covered lay-offs, 16 percent plant shutdowns, and 17 percent technological change.

Extended Vacations and Transfer Rights

Extended vacations can create job openings or prevent lay-offs. Some employees are given the option of transferring to another company plant. Transferred workers often receive relocation aid and usually have their previous seniority rights and company benefits maintained at the new plant. Transfer rights and/or relocation allowances are included in 43 percent of all agreements.

Management Restrictions

Some agreements contain clauses giving unions influence over the rate of labor-displacing technological change. Management is often prohibited from actions that threaten the job security of employees, such as subcontracting. Subcontracting is limited or prohibited in over half of all labor contracts. Subcontracting is normally permitted only when the necessary tasks cannot be completed in the factory and only after notification of the union. Controls are also negotiated to regulate overtime, crew size, and the work by nonunion management personnel. Almost all agreements (80 percent) contain one or more of these clauses. Two-thirds of the workers covered by major collective bargaining agreements have subcontracting protections.

Reduced Work Hours

Demand downturns may cause employers to shorten the work day and/or work week to maximize employment. Some contracts guarantee weekly income or a minimum number of hours of work. Work sharing maintains employment by reducing hours of individual workers so that two employees fill one job. Most work sharing and shortened work week provisions limit the reduction of work hours to no less than thirty-two hours weekly.

Work sharing is permitted by seven percent and a reduction of hours by 18 percent of the agreements. Almost 2 million workers are covered by work sharing.

Wage Maintenance

Twelve percent of all agreements guarantee a weekly, monthly, or annual wage. The majority of these agreements guarantee a weekly wage regardless of hours worked, normally thirty-six to forty paid hours each week.

Recall and Rehire

Most employers recall workers according to seniority lists. Some employers maintain lists of discharged employees who enjoy recall priority. Management sometimes uses the list to assist laid-off employees to find employment outside the company.[23]

Seventy-one percent of the agreements contain provisions preserving seniority rights during lay-offs for some 5.2 million employees. The retention of seniority rights ranges from less than six months to more than five years. The most common length is one year (19 percent) or a period equal to or proportional to length of service (21 percent).

Retraining

Agreements often offer retraining to employees whose position has been eliminated because of technological changes. Retraining programs permit displaced workers to learn how to operate new equipment or to take jobs in other sections of the plant. Costs are often absorbed by the company and can result in a pay increase for the employee. Some contracts provide financial support for training that prepares a displaced worker for employment elsewhere.

On-the-job training is included in 37 percent of the agreements. Apprenticeship programs, including formal off-the-job training, are provided by 43 percent. The cost of tuition for job-related training is paid in part or completely in 5 percent of the agreements.

Severance Pay

Monetary assistance is most common in the event of permanent displacement or if lay-offs last more than two years. Severance pay is required by 32 percent of all agreements and covers 38 percent of the work force. Severange pay is usually lump-sum compensation for termination of employment. The amount is sometimes based on length of service.

Supplemental Unemployment Benefits

SUB payments are employer-paid benefits that supplement regular UI payments. First negotiated in the 1956 Ford-United Auto Worker (UAW) agreement, SUB programs now cover about two million auto, steel, and rubber workers. SUB payments bring the gross base pay of laid-off workers up to a fixed fraction of previous wages (usually 80 to 95 percent) and normally tie the length of SUB benefits to an unemployed worker's length of service. SUB benefits are taxable, but regular UI benefits are not. In 1980, about 14 percent of all major collective bargaining agreements had SUB provisions covering 2 million workers.

   The first SUB agreement was a response to the decline in the average weekly wage-replacement rate under regular UI to 32 percent in 1951. SUB benefits are most often provided "in those industries where companies want to retain access to a trained labor force following periods of high unemployment."[24] SUBs are most common in the auto industry—auto SUB programs pay about three-fourths of all SUB benefits.[25] The auto industry has a special SUB, a guaranteed benefit account, that supplements UI payments to workers with ten or more years seniority regardless of the state of a company's regular SUB account. The cyclical sheet-metal industry finances a SUB that provides up to 4.5 weeks wages to union members who worked less than the average length of employment in the preceding six months. This SUB also pays up to $750 travel costs to encourage unemployed union members to take temporary jobs in areas with too few sheet-metal workers.

Specially Negotiated Agreements

Specially negotiated agreements govern the introduction of and compensation for large-scale labor displacement, usually the displacement resulting from technological changes. Most technological changes occur without union restrictions, in part because many changes occur outside the industry where their labor-displacing impacts are felt. For example, can and paper containers eliminate bottle-making jobs and reduce the number of materials-handling jobs, but the bottle-makers union can do little to control the use of paper containers. Union policies vis-à-vis technological changes fall into five overlapping categories: willing acceptance; opposition; competition (keeping the old way in use);

encouragement of new methods; and adjustment to changes. Sumner Slichter argued that the nature of the union and the firm involved and the technological change itself largely determined union policies toward change.[26] Generally, craft unions facing large-scale lay-offs in declining industries resist change most; as, for example, railroad unions that protect redundant firemen on diesel locomotives.

Unions adjusting to technological change sometimes negotiate ad hoc agreements regulating dismissals that provide compensation and other services to displaced workers. Since each technological change is unique, specially negotiated agreements are tailor-made for specific displacement situations. Most agreements combine a variety of general adjustment provisions in combination to cushion the effects of large-scale labor displacement. Railroads, for example, tried to eliminate firemen on diesel locomotives for years before reaching agreement in 1963 to phase out firemen through attrition. Since labor is usually half a railroad's operating costs, railroad management continues to press for crew size reductions, such as one or no brakeman to assist the engineer and conductor in the current four person train crew. Railroads argue that deregulation forces them to cut costs to compete with trucks; unions counter that the brakemen are needed for safety reasons. A similar cost-reduction versus safety fight is brewing over the proposed move from three to two-person cockpit crews in new airliners.

The 1960 Mechanization and Modernization Agreement between West Coast Longshoremen and the Pacific Maritime Association (PMA) assisted workers displaced by the switch to container-handling of freight. The International Longshoreman's and Warehousemen's Union (ILWU) resisted the containerization of cargo handling for years. Under the agreement PMA bought out the job property rights that noncontainer work rules had created. The ILWU gave up its rules in exchange for a guarantee that no member of the preferred class of longshoremen, the fully registered union members, would be laid off as a result of containerization. Employers agreed to contribute $29 million over a five and one-half year period to a trust fund established to finance new and improved benefits for fully registered longshoremen. The benefits included a guaranteed average weekly wage (which the union considered to be the sale price of workers' property rights), early retirement and increased retirement, disability, and death benefits, a payment for the workers' share of the machine. East Coast longshoremen are guaranteed $20,000 annually (1979)—regardless of actual hours worked—as compensation for the ILA's acceptance of containers. Even with these job protections, ILA membership has been reduced to 15,000 members from 25,000 in 1965.

Longshoremen are fighting for the right to handle all maritime freight containers within fifty miles of a port. The National Labor Relations Board (NLRB) ruled that an agreement between the ILA and the shipping industry granting such packing and unpacking container work to longshoremen was not valid because the union was trying to acquire the work traditionally done by freight consolidators and trucking companies. The Supreme Court reversed the NLRB in

1980 and ordered the NLRB to reexamine the ILA agreement. The Supreme Court held in a five to four ruling that the work preservation doctrine protects union activities that "attempt to accommodate change while preserving as much of [the union's] traditional work as possible."[27] The Supreme Court will apparently approve agreements that preserve the same generic type of work—not just exact work patterns—even if the way work is preserved is not the "most rational or efficient response to innovation."[28]

Railroads are another sector threatened with labor displacement because of technological changes, railroad mergers, and more recently competition from deregulated trucks. The May 1936 Washington Job Protection Agreement—still in effect—protects workers affected by the coordination of railroad facilities or operations. It guarantees displaced workers a Monthly Dismissal Allowance (MDA) of 60 percent of a worker's previous monthly earnings for up to five years. Instead of the MDA, a displaced worker can take a lump-sum severance allowance of up to twelve months pay.[29]

Workers who retained their jobs but were bumped into lower-paying positions are eligible for an MDA that assures them their original monthly earnings for up to five years. Employees required to move are entitled to moving-expense reimbursement and compensation for the loss suffered in selling a house. Displaced employees retain fringe benefits as long as they remain available for railroad work.

Rail unions have negotiated work rules that effectively guarantee lifetime jobs. However, some railroads go bankrupt, and unions must negotiate severance pay. Rail unions, including the Brotherhood of Railway and Airline Clerks (BRAC), obtained lump-sum payments of $2,000 for each year of service (up to $25,000) from the Milwaukee Road's creditors to aid displaced workers, but got nothing from purchasers of the Rock Island Line, which employed 8,700 workers when it went bankrupt in September 1979. In the Rock Island case, BRAC allowed "the purchaser of a bankrupt line to ignore past labor ogligations and hire only those employees needed for operations."[30] Congress enacted the Rock Island Employees and Transition Act in 1980 requiring the Rock Island's bankruptcy trustee to provide benefits to 5,000 formerly employed workers by getting a federal loan of $75 million to be repaid from the railroad's estate. After a reorganization court refused to implement the labor protection clauses of the Act, the Supreme Court agreed that this ex post compensation violates the Fifth Amendment's ban on taking private property from the estate unlawfully and denied the workers any severance benefits.[31]

Hormel, a meat-packing company, negotiated an agreement that guaranteed employment, minimum weekly wages, and fifty-two weeks advance notice of lay-offs, effective on the first day of employment. The employees are in effect salaried, receiving a paycheck that does not fluctuate with the number of hours worked. Should the employee work over 2,080 hours for the year, the person receives payment for the hours above the minimum at the end of the year.

Excess wages do not have to be repaid, and overtime wages are not paid except under specific conditions.

A similar plan was negotiated by the *New York Times* and the International Typographical Union in 1974 to introduce labor-displacing printing equipment. Affected employees were guaranteed lifetime jobs or bonuses and other incentives if they opted for retirement or retraining.

The pace of labor-displacing technological change may accelerate because sharply higher energy prices have made some equipment prematurely obsolete just when liberalized investment tax credits and modified depreciation schedules lower the cost of new machinery. If employers want to replace equipment in existing unionized plants, they must bargain with unions beset by internal debates between the consequences of work preservation versus possible plant closure. Instead of negotiating special agreements, some employers simply close their plants and move production elsewhere.

Assessment

Collective bargaining is a flexible instrument that permits the workers and employers directly involved to resolve displacement trade-offs in tailor-made agreements. Most unions permit the employer to do what must be done to promote efficiency and profits but reserve the right to challenge management strategies if too many workers are being asked to pay too high a price. Strikes over job security are rare. Only 3 percent of the 4,230 strikes that began in 1978 involved job security issues. However, almost one-fourth of all workers on strike were involved in work stoppages where job security was a major issue. Most of these workers (82 percent) were protesting "new machinery or other technological issues."[32]

The cooperation common in the past may be threatened by the accelerated pace of plant closures in the basic steel, auto, and rubber industries and the tendency for multi-plant companies to open new (nonunion) plants in the South, West, or abroad. Cooperation is hampered by management attitudes that seek union-free environments and union convictions that the plant where it is entrenched will be closed in any event. In this atmosphere, collective bargaining is more likely to seek maximum assistance for displaced workers rather than jointly manage the introduction of efficiency-increasing change.

Indeed, most observers expect job security to be the issue in 1982 negotiations. Employer resistance to higher wages and high unemployment among union members is expected to reduce average wage increases from 11.5 percent in 1981 to 8.8 percent in 1982. The first major union to begin bargaining in 1982, the Oil, Chemical, and Atomic Workers (OCAW), demanded a two-year, no-lay-off clause and made it a top priority. This focus on job security is expected to hasten the shift from pattern-setting industrywide bargaining to plant-by-plant negotiations over job security.

The number and regional concentration of recent labor displacements have prompted attempts to enact federal job security protections. The Corporate Democracy Act of 1980, sponsored by Ralph Nader and several unions, would have required companies to give six months to two-years notice before closing plants. Employers believe advance notice denies them needed flexibility, because creditors and customers may start taking their business elsewhere, and because workers with no future are less productive. But advance notice can benefit employers by shocking workers into wage concessions or work-rule changes that increase productivity enough to keep the plant open. Even if dismissal is inevitable, workers are motivated to find another job since it is easier to maintain work habits and get references before a spell of unemployment benefits intervenes. Current practices might justify mandatory three to six months notice to balance the interests of labor and management.

Mandatory advance notice may presage the development of general job property rights. Other countries already guarantee lifetime employment for some workers (Japan) or require redundancy payments that can equal the remaining lifetime earnings of a dismissed worker (Belgium). In the United States, employee pension claims—the most valuable asset of most employees over fifty —are second only to taxes when making claims on the assets of a bankrupt firm (up to 30 percent of the firm's net worth).

Job property rights would add a fourth kind of asset to the traditional trilogy of real (land), personal (possessions), and intangible (patents) property.[33] A job property right is unique because it cannot be bought, sold, pawned, or bequeathed. Some labor lawyers believe that all workers are entitled to advance notice and/or justification for dismissal because of the constitution's due process and equal protection guarantees. Professor Peck, for example, argues that the explicit goal of full employment requires the " . . . observance of procedural due process guarantees, and that discharge without cause constitutes a deprivation of equal protection of the law to the unorganized employees of private employers."[34]

The most important elements in establishing job property rights include determination of how job property rights accumulate with an employee's tenure and how employers compensate dismissed workers for loss of accumulated rights. Two states have already passed weak versions of such laws. Maine's 1971 law pays one week's wages at dismissal for each year worked, while Wisconsin's 1975 plantclosing law requires sixty-day advance notice. State laws are seen by unions as a stopgap measure, since states may compete for new plants on the basis of their (easy) closure laws.

General job property rights would simplify but not eliminate bargaining over labor-displacing change.[35] Unless a uniform schedule of payments for job loss were prescribed, each dismissed employee's compensation would have to be determined by private, union, or public arrangements. Even if compensation were fixed externally, unions could still bargain over the pace of labor-displacing change, the impacts of new technology on other workers, and retraining options.

Mandatory advance notice and compensable job property rights would only modify current private protection arrangements.

One variation on proposals for advance notice and individual compensation is advance notice and compensation for communities affected by plant closures. The unions most affected by recent plant closures—the United Auto Workers (UAW), United Steel Workers, (USW), and International Association of Machinists (IAM)—seek the support of Snowbelt mayors, in Douglas Fraser's words, "to inject social responsibility" into plant closure decisions, and "to protect workers and communities against their devasting impact."[36] A 1980 proposal by Representative William Ford (D-Mich.) would have required six months' to two years' notice so that hearings to discuss company-prepared social impact statements could be held before an officer of the newly created National Employment Relocation Administration to see if plant closures were justified. Companies closing plants would be required to pay dismissed employees 85 percent of their average weekly earnings and reimburse communities for 85 percent of the first year's loss in tax revenues.

Collective bargaining is not the solution in every labor-displacing situation. First, negotiated agreements cover only about 25 percent of the nation's workers. Nonunion workers, especially those who work for the smaller companies with 100 or fewer employees that hire 60 percent of the United States work force, are not likely to receive advance notice or any other private job protections. In some instances, union resistance to labor-displacing change may perpetuate inefficient work rules and threaten the industry's viability. Finally, labor and management may have trouble making the necessary trade-offs in displacement situations if the cause of displacement is external, for example, imports or government actions. In these instances, labor and management may combine to resist rather than accommodate change.

Summary

U.S. workers have no general statutory protection from dismissal. The most general job protection available to workers is a tight labor market that encourages employers to retain employees whenever possible and expedites reemployment for those displaced. Civil rights, labor, and pension laws are creating indirect job property rights for some workers, but most do not receive compensation or employer-paid services after being dismissed.

Laid-off workers rely on both private and public resources to cushion their unemployment. The traditional private resource is personal savings, which is often too low to sustain most unemployed workers for more than a few weeks. A growing private resource is a working spouse. More husband-wife families have two earners (56 percent) than have just one earner (44 percent). In 1980, 60 percent of the unemployed lived in familities with at least one other wage earner,[37] and even in 1982, 40 percent of the unemployed live in families with incomes of twenty thousand dollars or more. If one spouse is unemployed, the other's income and fringe benefits help maintain living standards.

Displaced workers are also covered by the nation's general income security system. The first line of defense is unemployment insurance, the forty-five-year old earnings replacement program that pays an average of 42 percent of previous wages for six months. UI is often supplemented with in-kind food stamp benefits, one of the essential service programs. Few displaced workers fall back on income support or public assistance programs meant to bring incomes up to satisfactory levels.

Public unemployment assistance is often supplemented with private aid. Most private displacement protections are included in the collective bargaining agreements covering 25 percent of the nation's wage and salary workers. The most common benefits for short-term lay-offs are supplemental unemployment benefits, maintenance of fringe benefits, and seniority recall rights. Permanently displaced workers usually obtain short-term benefits, often receive advance notice, and are sometimes retrained for new jobs. More and more workers have their pensions vested after short-periods of employment, meaning that a pension is not lost because of displacement.

Technological changes are not usually opposed by unions. If a large number of workers are to be displaced, unions sometimes negotiate special agreements that compensate displaced workers. Recent plant closings have caused more problems because many firms reopen new plants in nonunion areas or abroad. Unions have pressed for federal regulation of plant closures.

Notes

1. *Payne* v. *Western & A.R.R.,* 81 Tenn. 507,51920 (1884), *overruled on other grounds,* quoted in Blades, "Employment at Will vs. Individual Freedom: On Limiting the Abusive Exercise of Employer Power, *Columbia Law Review* 67(1967):1405. For more recent judicial expressions of the same principle, see Weyand, "Present Status of Individual Employee Rights," 22 *New York University Conference on Labor* 171, 175 no. 15 (1969).

2. "Plant Closures," *The Economist,* January 10, 1981, p. 24.

3. The Supreme Court concluded in First National Maintenance Corp. v. NLRB, argued in 1981, that the initial decision to close a plant is *not* a mandatory subject for bargaining.

4. See Clyde Summers, "Individual Protection Against Unjust Dismissal: Time for a Statute," *Virginia Law Review* 62(1976):486; Cornelius Peck, "Unjust Discharges from Employment: A Necessary Change in the Law," *Ohio State Law Journal* 40, no. 1 (1979):4–49; and Mary Glendon and Edward Lev, "Changes in the Bonding of the Employment Relationship: An Essay on the New Property," *Boston College Law Review* 20, no. 3 (1979):457–84.

5. "The Growing Cost of Firing Non-Union Workers," *Business Week,* April 6, 1981, p. 95.

6. Ibid., p. 98.

7. *Wall Street Journal,* October 13, 1981, p. 1. A *Business Week* editorial criticized the practice of granting generous termination allowances to executives forced out of management. RCA paid President Maurice Valente $1.25 million to get his resignation and $705,000 to remove Jane Pheiffer as head of NBC. A. Robert Abboud's July 1980 separation agreement with First Chicago Corp. paid him a lump-sum of $781,349 and an annual pension of $106,297. See "Cushioning the Fall," *Business Week,* March 30, 1981, p. 150. European executives also collect severance pay—up to five years salary in Germany and Belgium.

8. Three states—Alabama, Alaska, and New Jsesey—also require employees to make UI contributions.

9. Most UI recipients are receiving either regular state (twenty-six weeks) or extended federal (thirteen weeks) UI benefits. In December 1980, 97 percent of the four million UI recipients were receiving these benefits—only three percent were federal employees, newly discharged veterans, or railroad retirement board UI beneficiaries.

10. Farmworkers must be covered in all stages by farmers who hire ten or more workers in twenty weeks or have at least a $20,000 quarterly payroll. Household workers are covered if at least $1,000 is spent on household services in one quarter. States can elect more inclusive definitions. California, for example, requires UI coverage of all employees if the quarterly payroll exceeds $100.

11. Raymond Munts finds the underlying rationale for this exclusion slightly muddy. Work histories are justified so that "the unemployed individual demonstrates that he is 'insured' under the system and entitled to benefits" or because "a record of recent work . . . adds to the presumption that the applicant is work-oriented." "Policy Development in Unemployment Insurance," Goldberg et al., *Federal Policies and Worker Status Since the Thirties* (Madison: Industrial Relations Research Association, 1976), p. 90.

12. Department of Labor (DOL) News Release, March 13, 1981.

13. Mr. James Van Erden of DOL's UI service estimated that extended benefits would cost $10 billion annually if the unemployment rate reached 9 percent, as it did in 1975. See Philip Shabecoff, "Reagan Seeks Tighter Work Test for Those on Extra Unemployment Benefits," *New York Times,* April 8, 1981, p. A22.

14. Neil Chamberlin et al., *The Labor Sector* (New York: McGraw Hill, 1980), p. 503.

15. Martin Feldstein, "Unemployment Compensation: Adverse Incentives and Distributional Anomalies," *National Tax Journal,* June 1974, estimated that UI replaces an average 46 to 78 percent of previous after tax earnings. These estimates do not consider the value of lost fringe benefits. A 1980 study by

Daniel Hamermesh found that about half the UI recipients spend UI benefits just like other income (that is, not just on necessities), a finding some observers believe should justify taxing all UI benefits to increase government revenues about $3 billion annually.

16. *Wall Street Journal,* January 16, 1979, p. 1.

17. Munts, *Federal Policies,* p. 100.

18. Ibid., p. 91. Unavailability for work disqualified 32 percent of rejected UI applicants, closely followed by leaving one's job without good cause. A DOL study apparently found considerable numbers of UI recipients unable or unavailable for work. One-fourth of the average 12.6 percent UI overpayments in six cities went to workers who failed to conduct mandatory active job searches. *Wall Street Journal,* January 29, 1981, p. 44.

19. Peter Henle, "Exploring the Distribution of Earned Income," *Monthly Labor Review,* December 1972, pp. 16–27.

20. S. Slichter et al., *The Impact of Collective Bargaining on Management* (Washington: The Brookings Institution, 1960), especially chapter 12.

21. *Characteristics of Major Collective Bargaining Agreements* (Washington: Bureau of Labor Statistics, 1980), Bulletin 2065.

22. The United Rubber Workers' contracts require rubber companies closing plants to give at least six months notice and to agree that "if not able to reach agreement on saving the plant, company and union will negotiate as to method and rules for closing the plant."

23. Scott Paper Company spent $1,000 mailing letters to local employers praising "the Scott workers' skills and productivity" in an effort o help 400 employees displaced from its Sandusky, Ohio plant in December 1980 find new jobs. Only one-third of the displaced workers found new jobs within four months, and several had to accept pay cuts. *Wall Street Journal,* February 10, 1981, p. 1.

24. Munts, *Federal Policies,* p. 80, notes that SUB "also drew unions and companies away from efforts to improve unemployment insurance legislation."

25. Margaret Yeo, "Company-Paid Plans Aid Laid-Off Workers in Some Big Industries," *Wall Street Journal,* January 2, 1980, p. 1.

26. Slichter, *Impact of Collective Bargaining,* p. 344.

27. NLRB v. International Longshoremen's Association, 48 U.S.L.W. 4765 (June 20, 1980).

28. Ibid., Justice Marshall's footnote 27, p. 4,771.

29. The evolution of private and public job protections is described in chapter 7 of U.S. Railway Association (USRA). *Conrail at the Crossroads* (Washington: USRA, 1981).

30. Leslie Wayne, "Time Running Out for Conrail," *New York Times,* April 19, 1981, p. F13.

31. "Justices to Study Limit to Helping Ex-Rail Workers," *Wall Street Journal,* April 28, 1981, p. 9.

32. *Work Stoppages* (Washington: BLS Bulletin 2066, June 1980), table 11.

33. Peter Drucker, "The Job as Property Right, *Wall Street Journal,* March 4, 1980.

34. Peck, "Unjust Discharges" p. 4.

35. Legislative and legal battles are now underway to extend job property rights to farmworkers threatened by displacement when farmers adopt privately built machines originally developed by publicly supported land-grant universities. California Rural Legal Assistance sued the University of California for unlawfully subsidizing the development of labor-saving machines that benefit only a few (large) farmers. Secretary of Agriculture Bergland embraced the suggestion that federal funds should not be used to develop labor-saving machines where "the major effect of the research will be the replacing of an adequate and willing workforce with machines." See R. Lindsey, "Coast Farm Workers Score Gain in Their Job Fight with Machines," *New York Times,* February 11, 1980.

36. Quoted in James Singer, "A Radical Solution to the Problem of Runaway Plants," *National Journal,* June 23, 1979, p. 1,040.

37. D. Westcott and R. Bednarzik, "Employment and Unemployment: A Report on 1980," *Monthly Labor Review,* February 1981, pp. 4–14.

4 Special Protection Programs

Special protection programs (SPPs) compensate displaced workers for loss of seniority and specific job skills when a federal government action causes unemployment. SPPs partially replace lost earnings with weekly payments that supplement regular UI benefits and provide a variety of adjustment assistance services including counseling, retraining, and relocation aid. There are about twenty of these programs,[1] most created in the 1970s. Imprecision results from the fact that some of the programs have not yet paid any benefits and because some SPPs permit displaced workers to ask for administrative help but do not guarantee cash benefits.

SPPs are divided into five categories. SPPs have for over forty-five years compensated and assisted railroad workers displaced by private or public rail reorganization. Since 1964 workers displaced because of federally funded mass-transit improvements have been entitled to compensation and assistance, as have workers displaced by airline deregulation since 1978. The number of potential transportation SPP beneficiaries is usually known before the first payments are made; hence, transportation SPPs are theoretically close-ended programs.

Trade adjustment assistance (TAA) is the largest single open-ended SPP. TAA benefits supplement UI and can subsidize the retraining and relocation of workers partially or totally displaced when increased imports are deemed to have contributed importantly to decreased production and lay-offs. The original 1962 TAA program limited eligibility for benefits to displaced workers whose unemployment was chiefly caused by imports. A 1974 revision liberalized eligibility criteria. TAA costs ballooned to a projected $2.7 billion in FY 1981 (table 4-1), but were cut sharply in FY 1982.

The Redwoods Employee Protection Program (REPP) is an example of a close-ended special loss compensation program, similar to transportation SPPs because its benefits are confined to a specific industry and the number and identity of potential beneficiaries is known before the first payment is made. Like the Juvenile Justice SPP, the Redwoods program acknowledges that workers will be displaced through no fault of their own as society pursues a nonemployment goal, for example, halfway houses instead of incarceration or preservation of redwoods for future generations. Special loss compensation SPPs often provide more generous benefits to displaced workers than other SPPs.

Disaster relief programs permit persons made unemployed by presidentially declared disasters to receive payments equivalent to regular UI benefits for up to one year regardless of the state's UI eligiblity requirements. Disaster relief

61

Table 4–1
Trade Adjustment Assistance Outlays and Recipients
(millions of dollars)

		Number of Recipients
TQ (July to September 1975)	34.0	27,258
Fiscal year 1976	69.9	46,824
Fiscal year 1977	150.9	110,702
Fiscal year 1978	258.3	156,599
Fiscal year 1979	258.5	131,722
Fiscal year 1980	1,624.5	536,086
Fiscal year 1981 (projected)	2,700.00	–

Source: International Labor Affairs Bureau (ILAB), U.S. Department of Labor (Washington: ILAB, January 19, 1981).

allows the president to override a state's normal eligibility criteria and to make the equivalent UI, food stamp, and other public benefits available to disaster victims. Disaster relief SPPs are the only SPPs that do not compensate workers for federally caused unemployment.

The water and air pollution control acts require the Environmental Protection Agency (EPA) administrator to investigate the employment impacts of issuing effluent limitation regulations at the request of adversely affected workers. The EPA administrator must consider employment impacts and make "such recommendations as he deems appropriate," but the EPA administrator is not required or authorized "to modify or withdraw any effluent limitation or order issued under this Act." This mandatory consideration of employment effects is the weakest special federal job protection.

The five types of SPPs—transportation, open-ended, special loss compensation, regular UI benefits, and consideration—create job property rights for workers unemployed for specific reasons. Other employment and labor laws create a different kind of compensable job property right for workers dismissed, demoted, or not hired. Workers unlawfully dismissed for union activities or because of their race, age, sex, national origin, religion, and, in some localities, sexual preference may be entitled to reinstatement and back wages. Similarly, workers dismissed or demoted for filing complaints with environmental, health, safety, or equal employment opportunity agencies may be reinstated with back pay.

The job property rights arising from unlawful employer actions are fundamentally different from those created by SPPs. SPPs distribute federal tax revenues to persons adversely affected by government actions; employment laws require employers to compensate workers if employers violate a law.

Before examining the five types of SPPs, it will be helpful to make some general comparisons between SPPs and UI.

Comparing Special Protection Programs and Unemployment Insurance

SPPs compensate workers who lose their jobs or careers when a federal government action or policy reduces employment in an industry or area. State UI laws, on the other hand, seek to partially replace wages for all workers subject to the risk of involuntary unemployment. Different purposes mean that SPPs differ from UI in coverage, eligibility, and benefits.

UI coverage has been extended by adding more employers and employment subject to the federal unemployment tax. If states do not cover such employers in their UI systems, employers do not get credit for the state UI taxes they pay into state UI funds and must still pay a 3.4 percent federal UI tax. While federal and state laws seek to make UI coverage universal, SPPs ask only if a totally or partially unemployed worker was employed in an industry or job protected by an SPP and displaced by a federal action or policy.

Eligibility for UI is contingent on a record of substantial employment (at least fourteen to twenty weeks of work) over the previous 12-month base period. Qualifying UI employment need not be with a specific employer or in a particular industry. UI benefits depend on previous earnings and continue (up to a maximum number of weeks) so long as a person is unemployed, able to work, and available for suitable work.

Under SPPs, a worker need not be unemployed to receive benefits. SPPs do not limit benefits (as does UI) to those unemployed because no suitable work is available. Under the transportation, TAA, Redwoods Employee Protection Program (REPP), and several other SPPs, a worker can remain working full time at a subnormal wage and receive partial SPP benefits. Some SPPs link the level of benefits to years of service, but most SPPs simply require workers to be employed in a specific industry at a particular time to be eligible for benefits. Benefits continue for definite time periods or until a worker has either found or refused suitable alternative work.

SPPs aim to restore an affected worker to the status he had before a government action dislocated him. SPP benefits are usually more generous than UI payments. UI aims to replace enough of a worker's lost earnings to cover nondeferrable expenses and not force the exhaustion of savings. The workable definition of UI benefit adequacy is a benefit of at least half an unemployed worker's normal weekly wage. UI benefits depend on past wages and continue long enough to enable most unemployed workers to find new jobs before their benefits are exhausted, usually twenty-six weeks. Most states limit the benefit period for workers with only few weeks of work during the base period, but eleven states permit all eligible workers to claim maximum benefits under the principle that full protection depends on eligibility, not how long contributions have been made.[2]

SPP benefits both restore and indemnify displaced workers. The addition of indemnification means that benefit levels are not designed to preserve work incentives. SPP benefits are normally paid weekly, although some SPPs permit a one-time lump-sum compensation payment. In addition to cash assistance, some SPPs offer retraining and relocation subsidies. Since SPPs are concerned more with reparation than work incentives, SPPs pay benefits for longer periods of time: up to six years under REPP or until age sixty-five for Conrail employees with five or more years of service.

Transportation

Railroad employees have been protected from displacement caused by mergers since 1933, when the Emergency Railroad Transportation Act ordered rail carriers to maintain employment at their May 1933 levels and to pay the moving costs of all employees required to relocate. In 1940, the Interstate Commerce Act was amended by Section 5(2)(f) to require the Interstate Commerce Commission (ICC) to make labor protection a condition for approving rail mergers, consolidations, acquisitions, and line abandonments. The ICC promulgated its labor protections in the *New Orleans Conditions* of 1952.[3] These labor protections were based on the privately negotiated Washington Job Protection Agreement of 1936.

Under the New Orleans Conditions, workers are protected for at least four years from the date that the ICC approves a rail merger or acquisition. During this four year period, a laid-off worker receives a monthly dismissal allowance (MDA) that equals the worker's previous average monthly earnings. Workers bumped into lower-paying jobs get an MDA that keeps monthly earnings at their original level. In addition, workers required to relocate are reimbursed for moving costs and losses incurred in selling and buying a house.

Federal job protections have often been supplemented by negotiated private protections. Several railroads, including the Penn Central, Norfolk and Western, and Burlington Northern, have agreed to reduce employment in some jobs only through attrition. These attrition agreements effectively guarantee certain workers lifetime jobs.

The Urban Mass Transit Act (UMTA) of 1964 extended job protection to 180,000 transit workers who may be affected if states and cities obtain federal funds to revamp their urban transit systems. Before a state or city can receive a UMTA loan, the secretary of transportation must certify that fair and equitable arrangements have been made to protect mass-transit employees. The

UMTA's Section 13(d) provides that these arrangements should be comparable to those established for railroad employees. All those employed when the city or state makes its application for federal funds are guaranteed continued employment at their old wage for at least four years. Workers made redundant continue to receive wages and maintain their pension and seniority rights while undergoing retraining.

The Regional-Rail Reorganization Act (1973), as amended in 1976, protects workers employed by the six northeastern and midwestern railroads that were consolidated to form Conrail in 1976. Conrail is a for-profit rail corporation meant to restructure bankrupt railroads into an economically viable rail system. Contrail is the nation's second largest freight carrier, employing 57,000 persons in 1981 to move freight over 17,700 miles of track. In 1981, Conrail revenue topped $4.2 billion, the highest in the rail industry. Conrail's labor costs (fifty-one cents of every dollar of revenue) are higher than the industry average of forty-eight cents.[4]

Labor costs are high because the legislation establishing Conrail guaranteed lifetime job protection to the 45,000 workers who had been employed for at least five years by the six railroads in January 2, 1974. These protections cover about 60 percent of Conrail's 67,000 workers (57,000 freight workers and 10,000 passenger service workers).

Protected workers are entitled to maintenance of their old job or an equivalent position elsewhere. If business declines and a worker is downgraded to a lower paying job, he continues to receive his original salary. If no job is available, redundant workers receive a monthly displacement allowance that supplements UI and other earnings to bring total monthly earnings up to average monthly earnings (including overtime pay until October 1, 1980) over the twelve months preceding the establishment of Conrail. In 1980, the 1,700 laid-off workers obtained average annual payments of $28,800.[5] Eligible workers continue to draw the MDA payment until age sixty-five, when regular railroad retirement benefits begin. Instead of MDA and maintenance of seniority rights, a displaced worker may accept a lump-sum separation allowance of up to $20,000 and relinquish all other job protection rights.

Conrail labor protections are contained in Title V of the 1973 Rail Reorganization Act. "Title V was passed in response to rail labor's request that Congress provide for labor protection in exchange for labor's endorsement of Conrail, and in recognition of the labor protection already enjoyed by most employees of the Penn Central and Erie Lackawanna railroads ... [Title V] became the most expensive labor protection provision in labor history."[6] The cost of this labor protection figures prominently in discussions about the future of Conrail.

Conrail displacement benefits currently cost the federal government about $4 million monthly—$319 million since Conrail began. After the $485 million federal fund to pay these benefits is exhausted, Conrail is required to continue paying benefits to displaced workers that could total $2 to $4 billion. In 1981 bargaining, Conrail management argued successfully that 10,000 workers, including 4,600 excess brakemen and firemen, would have to be dismissed. Fred Knoll, the late president of the Brotherhood of Railway and Airline Clerks (BRAC) agreed to these lay-off concessions after receiving assurances that Conral will not be parcelled out to private railroads immediately.

Conrail was not profitable until 1981, when it earned a $39.2 million profit. From 1976 through 1980, Conrail received $3.3 billion in federal subsidies— $1.8 million each day. The Reagan administration urged Congress to halt federal payment to Conrail after a $300 million payment for FY 1981, arguing that the needed segments of Conrail will be continued by private enterprise. Deregulation of rail rates in 1980 has already prompted mergers among the eleven largest private railroads into five super railroads. Since few observers believe that these private railroads will buy even part of Conrail unless job guarantees are weakened, the Reagan administration proposed a doubling of the $200 million severance fund to make lump-sum payments to workers voluntarily leaving Conrail. Even with severance-accelerated quits, selling Conrail to private railroads is expected to displace 17,000 to 40,000 workers.[7]

Studies released in April 1981 by the Department of Transportation, Conrail, and the U.S. Railway Association (USRA) argue that Conrail's labor protections must be reduced. The USRA report concludes that "the lifetime protection guarantees of Title V have proven a costly error that imposes enormous costs on taxpayers. Title V enables surplus protected employees to sit at home collecting labor protection (payments) until they are eligible for railroad retirement."[8] The USRA report criticizes the continuance of protection until age sixty-five because it does not encourage workers to take lump-sum severance. By USRA's reckoning, Conrail has 1,100 protected workers between thirty-one and thirty-four whose lifetime protection would cost $800,000 each in 1980 dollars. USRA wants to modify labor protections and have the federal government continue paying for them.

The twenty-five unions that represented Conrail workers in 1981 negotiations agreed to some work-rule changes and a deferral of wage increases that saved Conrail $150 million in 1981. But the United Transportation Union (UTU) is becoming uneasy because Conrail has begun to eliminate jobs that had been held by workers who accepted lump-sum severance payments. Conrail and its unions are trying to adjust and preserve the rail system, but the question hanging over both Conrail and its unions is whether Conrail will be sold immediately or given several more years to become profitable.

The Rail Passenger Service Act (1970) maintains the jobs and privileges of about 18,000 workers employed by the thirteen passenger railroads which terminated inter-city passenger service upon creation of Amtrak. Workers employed in 1970 continue to receive their old wages, including any increases negotiated in subsequent collective bargaining agreements, for six years from the date they become adversely affected. Some Amtrak workers retain seniority with the railroad that continues to pay them, since Amtrak reimburses rail carriers for operating its trains. Displaced workers are eligible for paid training and retraining. The National Railroad Passenger Service Corporation Assistance Act (1972) extended job protection to terminal and other service personnel.

Like Conrail, Amtrak has not been profitable. Amtrak got a federal subsidy of almost $1 billion in FY 1981, a subsidy that was reduced to $735 million in FY 1982. Echoing Conrail, Amtrak management insists that it requires a subsidy because of the expensive job protections granted workers when Amtrak was formed. The Senate Commerce Committee in April 1981 approved a bill that included a revised schedule of payments to displaced Amtrak workers that was estimated to save $75 million. The Reagan administration later urged local transportation authorities to take over Amtrak commuter service, but a 1982 plan to put former Amtrak and Conrail employees under New York's Taylor law that forbids strikes by public employees was rejected by the Supreme Court. In June 1982, Amtrak negotiated a thirty-nine month agreement with its fifteen unions that loosened work rules and is expected to save Amtrak $132 million over the next three years.

The High Speed Ground Transportation Act (1965) extends Amtrak-type employee protections to railroads that get federal funds to develop high-speed ground transportation systems. The Federal Highway Act (1973) permits the diversion of Highway Trust Funds to make urban mass-transit improvements but entitles currently employed transit workers to Amtrak-style protections.

Since the Civil Aeronautics Board had regulated the airline industry for forty years, Congress established a ten-year employee protection plan when it deregulated the airline industry in 1978. Section 43 of the Airline Deregulation Act (1978) protects persons who had been employed for at least four years in 1978 by an FAA-certified airline from job loss or demotion until 1989. Job protections include monthly payments to dismissed workers of up to six years, relocation assistance, and rehire priority with seniority rights from the old employer preserved when applying for a job with any other FAA carrier. Benefits are available to employees only if deregulation requires an airline to lay off at least 7.5 percent of its full-time employees in a twelve-month period. Between 1976 and 1980 trunk airline employment increased 14 percent, making the labor protections superfluous for the act's first two years. Even in mid-1982, when over forty-thousand airline employees were unemployed, the CAB and the Reagan administration resisted a Congressional push for airline-employee payments. If benefits are paid in the future, they will be drawn from a general fund account, the Airline Employees Protective Account.

Transportation SPPs are the most established federal job protections. Several factors combined to justify federal protection. Most railroad, transit, and airline employees were covered by collective bargaining agreements with job protections when the federal government made major changes in the industry. Government regulation of transportation industries for such a long time is seen as a form of employee protection that should not be abolished with deregulation.

Finally, the opposition of well-entrenched unions to changes that are in the public interest could only be bought off with generous SPPs.

Open-Ended Special Protection Programs

The Trade Act of 1974 is the most prominent federal job protection program, spending an estimated $2.7 billion in FY 1981 (instead of the $400 million maximum expected). Trade adjustment assistance (TAA) is available to all workers with at least six months' service who have been or will be totally or partially displaced (put on reduced hours) because of increased imports until October 1982. Affected workers, their union, or their employer petition the Secretary of Labor to be certified for TAA benefits. Department of Labor staff investigate displacement circumstances to determine if increased imports caused or contributed importantly to lay-offs. DOL certification depends on finding increased imports of competitive products, reduced sales or production, and actual or threatened lay-offs.

TAA benefits include cash allowances, training and counseling, and relocation allowances. Cash allowances ensure that a displaced worker receives 70 percent of his previous weekly wage, up to the national average weekly manufacturing wage ($289 in 1981). UI benefits reduce TAA allowances dollar for dollar.

Certified workers may receive TAA benefits for up to fifty-two weeks. If workers enroll in an approved training course, they are eligible for an additional twenty-six weeks of TAA allowances. Workers aged sixty or older may receive the additional twenty-six weeks of benefits without enrolling in a training course. However, no worker may receive more than seventy-eight weeks of TAA benefits.

TAA benefits and services are provided through each state's employment security (UI) offices. If the local employment service agrees that a displaced worker is unlikely to find a suitable job within commuting distance, the worker is eligible for a job search allowance of up to $500. If an import-displaced worker finds a job elsewhere, he may be reimbursed for 80 percent of his moving costs and receive a lump-sum payment of up to $500.

Trade adjustment assistance is controversial because its cost has increased so rapidly. From only $70 million in FY 1976, TAA costs jumped to $2.7 billion in FY 1981, a 3,700 percent increase in five years (table 4-1). Most of the increased costs of TAAs can be traced to auto-industry unemployment—70 percent of the 441,000 TAA recipients in April 1980 were auto workers.[9] TAA recipients in two states—Michigan and Ohio—got 60 percent of all TAA payments in the first five months of FY 1981. Between 1975 and 1981, unemployed auto workers got 72 percent of TAA benefits (table 4-2).

The current TAA program is a revision of a very restrictive 1962 provision of the Trade Expansion Act. Adjustment assistance benefits were considered

Table 4–2
Trade Adjustment Assistance Outlays by Industry

Industry	Workers	Benefits (millions of dollars)
Auto	685,066	$2,155.1
Steel	136,176	347.5
Apparel	144,923	183.8
Footwear	75,565	90.6
Electronics	58,373	87.2
Fabricated metals	29,105	69.3
Textiles	25,827	43.1
Coal	4,605	17.7
		$2,994.3

Source: International Labor Affairs Bureau (ILAB), U.S. Department of Labor (Washington: ILAB, 1981).
Note: Cumulative totals, April 1975 to May 31, 1981.

better than escape-clause relief from imports (cases where the International Trade Commission agrees that imports are the most important cause of serious injury to an industry and imposes quotas on imports) because adjustment assistance got workers out of dying industries. The original TEA provisions were interpreted so narrowly that only 40,000 workers got $86 million between 1962 and 1975, when TAA replaced it.

TAA is justified on two grounds. First, covered unemployment is caused by federal trade policies and second, trade-caused unemployment "may be different in nature from unemployment that arises from other causes." The trade-unemployment link provides the equity rationale for TAA, but the nature of unemployment justification is more ambiguous. The Senate Finance Committee argued that trade-linked unemployment is different because entire industries may be adversely affected, meaning that workers with industry-specific skills suffer both earnings and accumulated skills losses. Further, trade-affected industries may be concentrated in a particular region. If so, the fact that many workers are made unemployed at once puts a strain on local labor markets.

TAA is the only SPP that has been studied extensively. Most of the first TAA studies complained of the administrative delays caused by certification—many benefit recipients were already back at work before they got their first TAA payments. However, one reason TAA recipients were back at work before receiving TAA checks was that many lay-offs proved to be only temporary. A major study of TAA benefit recipients found that because most TAA recipients were only on temporary lay-off, retraining and relocation services were seldom used (only 2 percent of the 500,000 TAA recipients in 1980 participated in training programs), and benefits usually arrived after the beneficiary was back at work. Administrative delays have been curbed, and it now appears that a higher fraction of TAA recipients may be permanently displaced.[10]

The most important conclusion that emerges from TAA studies is that it is very hard to predict the earnings losses caused by displacement. Much of the difficulty arises from the fact that many permanent dismissals wind up being only temporary lay-offs and vice versa. Since it is not clear that trade-displaced workers have suffered a permanent earnings loss when they are dismissed initially, the Reagan administration proposed in 1981 that TAA benefits be limited to those who have exhausted their regular UI benefits. In addition, TAA benefits were to be paid only at regular UI levels but be available for up to fifty-two weeks following regular UI benefit exhaustion.

Congress accepted these restrictions, in part because TAA benefits were not high enough to prevent the United Auto Workers union from pressing for protection from imports when one-third of its members were laid off. The Congressional Budget Office estimates that these changes could save $1.3 billion in FY 1982, almost 90 percent of the anticipated $1.5 billion cost of TAA.[11] The Department of Labor's preliminary FY 1983 budget anticipates spending only $112 million for TAA. Only TAA recipients already in training programs on July 1, 1982 would remain eligible for cash assistance; henceforth, workers displaced by imports would be eligible only for regular UI benefits.

Since the original Trade Expansion Act program was revised to TAA, many observers have pressed for coverage of workers indirectly dismissed by imports; employees of companies that supply parts or services to trade-impacted industries. It appeared such a bill would pass Congress in mid-1979, but budgetary concerns eventually killed it. TAA is now scheduled to expire in September 1982. Among the issues to be explored in reauthorization hearings are whether TAA should only be available to import-impacted workers only after regular UI benefits are exhausted (as in FY 1982) and whether TAA should put more emphasis on retraining and relocation. Business groups argue that TAA "should be reserved for painful adjustments forced by shifts in the patterns of trade,"[12] and not be used for temporary (auto) lay-offs. Labor still sees TAA as insufficient and often ineffective burial insurance, albeit better than nothing.

The TAA debate illustrates the issues implicit in all SPPs. Without generous TAA, trade-threatened workers will press for tariff and quota protection to preserve their jobs, increasing prices to consumers generally. In the summer of 1980, when 35 percent of the 800,000 U.S. auto workers were unemployed, a Carter administration task force estimated that limiting Japanese auto imports to 1979 levels (1.6 million autos) would create jobs for 100,000 unemployed auto workers but cost U.S. car buyers paying higher auto prices an additional $1 billion.[13] TAA, this argument runs, compensates the few whose unemployment lets everyone enjoy lower prices. The counter argument holds that a specific cause of unemployment (imports) is not a sufficient reason to pay extra unemployment benefits. Indeed, TAA opponents argue that the availability of

TAA ties workers to trade-vulnerable industries instead of encouraging them to seek jobs in other industries. Like many economic debates, TAA reform reveals the persistent efficiency (minimal TAA and rapid worker adjustment) and equity (generous TAA and slower adjustments) trade-off. The Reagan administration is stressing efficiency. Labor Secretary Donovan noted that "displaced auto workers unlikely to be hired in the near future will be encouraged to shift to other types of work, at entry levels if necessary,"[14] even if the worker has to take a 50 to 60 percent wage cut.

Special Loss Compensation

Special loss compensation programs require state and city applicants for federal social service funds to protect the jobs of persons employed at the time of application. The Juvenile Justice and Delinquency Prevention Act of 1974 provides funds to convert detention centers with guards into halfway houses with counselors. The job protections available under the act include transfer to another guard position with no loss of wages, conditions of work, or seniority rights, or a mutually agreeable compensation and retraining program. These job protections are similar to those available in the railroad industry.

The Special Health Revenue Sharing Act encourages states to treat the mentally ill in community health centers. States can obtain federal funds to build and operate such community centers. However, no grant may be made unless a state satisfies the Secretary of Health and Human Services that the currently employed workers of affected institutions will be protected.

The Developmental Disabilities Services and Facilities Construction Act as amended in 1975 encourages states to treat persons in community centers who suffer from disabling diseases contracted in childhood. If a grant to establish such a community center causes the total or partial closure of an institution, persons employed at the time of application must be offered job protections.

Special loss compensation programs create job property rights for state employees of service agencies applying for federal assistance. Since the agencies buy out these job property rights before their applications are approved, there is no readily available data on the number of persons affected and the cost of protecting them.

Workers displaced because defense contracts are cancelled are sometimes eligible for ad hoc special loss compensation. A House bill to require payments to such workers was introduced in 1979, but failed to gain Senate approval. The House did approve an experimental program to supplement the UI checks of persons laid off because of defense contract cancellations so that jobless workers would be assured $14,000 each for two years. This proposal failed to gain Senate concurrence.

The most controversial special loss compensation program is the Redwoods Employee Protection Program (REPP) established to compensate about 1,500 loggers affected by adding 48,000 acres to the Redwoods National Park (California) in 1978. REPP, the most complex SPP, has been labeled "the most lavish employee dislocation program in U.S. history."[15] It pays unemployed workers weekly benefits of up to $1,000 (although the average is about $300) or provides lump-sum severance payments that are often in the $30,000 to $50,000 range. REPP benefits are available for seven years (June 1977 through September 1984). As of September 1981, $40 million had been paid to displaced workers.

REPP was included in the Redwoods Park Expansion proposal after loggers and lumber companies protested that the newly protected acreage would displace workers and curtail business in a high-wage but isolated industry. Displaced workers have almost no chance to find similar work paying such high wages (up to $35 hourly for piece-rate tree fallers). A coalition of environmentalists, lumber companies, and workers joined to make REPP an integral part of the Redwoods Expansion Act.

A unique feature of REPP is presumptive certification. All covered employees totally or partially laid-off between May 31, 1977 and September 30, 1980 are conclusively presumed to have been laid off or placed on reduced hours because of Redwoods National Park expansion. Given the relatively small number of covered employees (1,500) and this automatic certification, two of the most common SPP problems—publicizing benefits and certifying eligibility—are not a REPP problem.

REPP benefits are comprehensive. Workers with five or more years of service are eligible for a weekly benefit equal to the highest wage earned between January 1, 1977 and March 21, 1978. This weekly cash benefit is reduced dollar for dollar if UI or social security is received or if a worker has some timber-related earnings. The weekly benefit is reduced by only fifty cents for each dollar earned outside timber to encourage loggers to explore new careers.

Weekly cash benefits are supplemented by continued health and social welfare program coverage and further accrual of pension rights. In addition, displaced redwoods workers are eligible for the vacation pay benefits they would have received if they had continued working. REPP benefits end in 1984, except for those fifty or older who may continue to draw benefits until age sixty-five.

Instead of weekly cash benefits, displaced workers may elect to receive a lump-sum severance payment. Severance pay is equal to one week's pay for every month of past employment up to a maximum of seventy-two weeks for six or more years of service. Most REPP severance payments are in the $20,000 to $40,000 range.

If the local employment service office determines that no suitable alternative job possibilities exist, a displaced redwoods worker may be retrained while receiving normal REPP benefits or receive a job search allowance of up to $500 and full moving reimbursement to leave the area for a new job elsewhere. Severance pay and relocation terminate eligibility for other REPP benefits.

Criticism of REPP is widespread. The deputy director of California's Employment Development Department, James Mattesich, criticizes REPP for being extremely complex and the displaced workers for doing "anything to obtain or maximize their benefits."[16] The fact that lay-offs are conclusively presumed to be the result of the expansion of the park is alleged to encourage employers to cooperate with workers, to lay off workers for two weeks at Christmas (1979), thus preserving the rights of these "affected workers . . . to collect benefits through 1984."[17] In April 1982, Secretary of Labor Donovan proposed new REPP rules that would limit benefits to persons who lost their jobs as a direct result of park expansion on or before December 31, 1978.

A very common view of REPP is that environmentalists formed a coalition with unionized loggers to preserve redwoods and to provide generous compensation to those displaced. However, the main author of REPP labor protections, Nat Weinberg, notes that REPP represents an honest attempt "to determine what is fair compensation for wages and benefits lost as a direct result of government action."[18] As long as special loss compensation protections are determined on an ad hoc basis, their varying provisions will seem unfair to some observers.

Criticism of generous REPP worker benefits may be misplaced. Three lumber companies—Louisiana-Pacific Corp (owner of 60 percent of the 48,000 acres added to the park), Arcata Corp, and Simpson Timber Company—have already received $300 million of a projected one billion dollars for the land they owned.[19] The original estimate of land settlement costs was $359 million. Company arguments that the land taken for the park is the most productive timberland in the world helped triple land acquisition costs and make the 1978 Redwood Park expansion the most expensive national park addition ever. A Reagan administration attempt to delay $21 million in land settlement payments was strongly opposed by the timber companies in Congress.

Disaster Benefits

The 1969 Disaster Relief Act (as amended in 1974) permits persons unemployed because of a presidentially declared disaster to collect weekly benefits equivalent to what the individual would have received under a state's normal UI program. If a disaster-displaced person is eligible for regular UI benefits, he must claim them and forfeit Disaster Unemployment Assistance (DUA).

DUA benefits are drawn from general revenues. Most disasters permit workers unemployed because of a catastrophe to draw DUA benefits for up to one year. However, the requirement that unemployed persons draw regular UI whenever possible means that a "large part of the cost of unemployment benefits in a disaster area is financed by the employer-taxed UI funds."[20] In FY 1979, 14,000 persons received $3.1 million in DUA unemployment payments, an average of $221 per unemployed person.

Amendments to the Public Works and Economic Development Act in 1974 allow payment of benefits to unemployed persons in areas experiencing actual or potential economic problems. Payments, up to maximum regular UI benefits, may continue for one year and be increased by rent supplements, mortgage payment aid, and relocation assistance. As of 1980 no benefits had yet been paid under this SPP.

Consideration

The weakest job protection provisions are those contained in air and water pollution control acts that require the Environmental Protection Agency (EPA) administrator to consider the employment effects of enforcing effluent regulations. Consideration allows workers and firms to publicize the employment impacts of enforcement, but the acts do not permit the EPA administrator to modify or withdraw effluent regulations because their enforcement will displace labor.

Some government employees have job property rights that require maintenance of their current salary for one or two years, even if the employee is demoted to a lower-paying job. During the FY 1982 reductions in force (RIF) caused by federal budget cuts, some high-wage employees had the option of accepting a much lower-graded job (but retaining their high salary for two years) or being laid off. The fact that federal workers receiving $50,000 a year can and do occupy $12,000 clerical jobs is said to reflect the federal government's inexperience "in laying off and firing its employees."[21] Some state and local government workers have similar retention of current salary rights.

The Role of Special Protection Programs

Most unemployment insurance experts have opposed the proliferation of SPPs. Their opposition reflects fears that giving extra benefits to some unemployed workers creates problems for the basic UI system. Almost all unemployed workers eligible for SPP and UI benefits are unemployed through no fault of their own. If involuntary unemployment is the basis for UI, the argument runs, then all unemployed workers would seem to have an equal claim on the resources available to assist the unemployed. This equal claim argument is undermined because most states link UI benefits to past employment and earnings records, so involuntary unemployment and a work history combine to determine the level and duration of benefits.

SPP critics have a more compelling argument when they note that SPP benefits are extended to only some of the victims of federal actions, for example, those adversely affected by trade policy but not energy or housing policies. The fact that the federal action-unemployment link is not clear-cut obscures causation but not workers' losses. Many workers are indirectly affected by federal actions. What claims do indirectly affected workers have on special job protection funds?

Troubling definitions that lead to seemingly arbitrary distinctions are compounded by the allegedly excessive benefits available under some SPPs. Conrail job protections and REPP are often singled out as SPPs that provide windfall benefits to lucky workers, not assistance that compensates and encourages retraining and relocation. Even though these SPPs affect relatively few workers, their generous benefits may undermine support for SPPs and UI generally.

The main defense of SPPs is that the regular UI system is designed to provide a basic protection against temporary unemployment and cannot cope with the unemployment resulting from some federal actions. SPPs are, in this view, a supplement to take pressure off of the regular UI system. Without SPPs, the UI system would be criticized for not assisting the workers the UI system was not designed to help.

The supplemental nature of SPPs is sometimes compared to the role of private SUB benefits that unions negotiate to bring unemployed workers' weekly payments up to some percentage of their normal weekly earnings. The difference between SUB and SPPs is that SUB is a private benefit, presumably obtained by workers who have traded increased wages or other benefits for extra payments during lay-offs. SPPs are a public supplement available to those workers able to negotiate extra benefits through the legislative process before a labor-displacing policy is enacted.

One troubling aspect of SPPs is a consistent failure to retrain and relocate experienced workers who are displaced. However, this shortcoming simply reflects the temporary nature of some lay-offs and the fact that employment and training programs are geared to serve groups that experience repeated and prolonged jobless spells. Manpower programs emerged to deal with the unemployment that was expected to afflict experienced workers in the early 1960s, but proved unnecessary for these workers. In the future, retraining and relocation programs for experienced workers may form an integral part of any industrial policy that helps specific industries adjust to economic change.

Summary

The federal government's twenty SPPs fall into the five general categories outlined in the appendix. These SPPs:

1. protect transportation workers employed before railroad consolidation, urban transit improvements, or airline deregulation takes effect;

2. provide open-ended assistance to workers partially or totally displaced by increased imports;

3. pay special loss compensation to a group of workers who will be displaced by pursuit of a nonemployment goal, for example, redwoods preservation and deinstitutionalization of the mentally ill;

4. override regular UI eligiblity criteria to compensate persons unemployed by a presidentially declared disaster;

5. require that the employment impacts of antipollution regulations receive consideration.

Job protections vary within and between these five categories. Generally, transportation and special loss compensation SPPs are most generous. All SPPs that pay benefits are more generous than regular UI. The TAA program spends more than any other SPP.

Federal SPPs are ad hoc responses to labor-displacing changes directly caused by federal actions or policies.[22] The fundamental question raised by these diverse SPPs is whether the United States should continue to establish supplemental job protection programs for specific groups of workers displaced by government actions or whether all existing SPPs should be folded into a reformed UI system. Before exploring the trade-offs between add-on SPPs and a single UI system, we examine European job protection programs.

Notes

1. Representative Sam Gibbons in *Examination of Special Jobless Benefit Programs* (Washington: Committee on Ways and Means, House of Representatives, 96th Congress, Second Session, February 21, 1980), p. 2.

2. This full protection principle covers those insured for fire—full protection does not depend on how long contributions have been made. See Murray Rubin, "The Proliferation of Special Employee Protection Programs," (Washington: National Commission on Unemployment Compensation, 1980), 3:793.

3. USRA, *Conrail*, pp. 47-8.

4. Leslie Wayne, "Time Running Out for Conrail," *New York Times*, April 19, 1981, p. F2.

5. Ibid, p. F13.

6. USRA, *Conrail*, p. 48.

7. Wayne, "Time Running Out for Conrail," p. F13.

8. USRA, *Conrail*, p. 51.

9. "The Upsurge in TAA," *The Morgan Guaranty Survey*, July 1980, p. 7. Many auto workers are covered by SUB plans that also supplement UI. If the unemployed workers are certified for TAA, these industry-financed SUB plans

are spared the need to make payouts. TAA also permits the commerce department to certify impacted firms for direct loans of up to $1 million and loan guarantees of up to $3 million. From 1975 through April 1980, 214 firms received $273 million.

10. Michael Aho and Thomas Bayard, "American TAA after Five Years," *The World Economy,* November 1980, p. 359.

11. Congressional Budget Office, *Reducing the Federal Budget: FY 1982-86* (Washington: CBO, 1981), p. 153.

12. *Business Week,* May 12, 1980, p. 144.

13. Clyde Farnsworth, "Carter Gets Car-Industry Aid Study," *New York Times,* July 3, 1980, p. 01.

14. Quoted in *Employment Relations Report,* March 25, 1981, p. 5.

15. John Berthllsen, "A Redwood Windfall," *Washington Post,* March 3, 1979, p. A-1.

16. Quoted in Representative Sam Gibbons, *Examination,* pp. 25-26.

17. Ibid, pp. 27-28.

18. Nat Weinberg, "Fairness for the Felled Loggers," *Washington Post,* March 31, 1979, p. A-14.

19. Pat Murkland, "National Park's Costs Grow," *Sacramento Bee,* April 12, 1981, p. AA9. The timber companies argue that the federal government should pay now to avoid expensive interest costs when they (eventually) win, as they did when the Redwoods Park was first created in 1968.

20. Mamoru Iohikawa, *Unemployment Insurance and Proliferation of Other Income Protection Programs for Experience Workers* (Washington: DOL, ETA, 1980), p. 19.

21. David Shribman, "Chopping the Federal Workforce," *New York Times,* November 8, 1981, p. F18.

22. Just how ad hoc these responses are is illustrated by the House Administration Committee's creation of sixty temporary jobs in the House clerk's office to aid staff members laid off by the unexpected elimination of the Select Committees on Population and Congressional Operations in 1979. *Washington Post,* April 12, 1979, p. A-7.

5 European Job Protections

European job protection programs reflect the influence of different economic structures; traditionally closer relationships between business, labor, and government; and tighter labor markets that reflect low birth rates and economic growth in the postwar period. Extensive laws and procedures governing lay-offs make worker dismissal an employer's privilege, not an automatic right. The result is a combination of collective bargaining protections and job security legislation that provide more benefits to more workers for longer periods than does the public-private U.S. system of job protections. U.S. unions insist that federal legislation to assure "comparable or better protection for American workers and communities is clearly feasible and long overdue."[1]

Most European economies are far more dependent on exports than the U.S. economy. The importance of international trade means that European economies have been buffeted by labor-displacing external shocks far longer than the U.S. economy. The frequent need for adjustments to both external and internal dislocations prompted early cooperation between government, labor, and business to cope with temporary and permanent dismissals. The fact that most European workers are union members and that their employers belong to strong employer associations permits industry-wide planning for economic dislocation with government encouragement and mediation, not the ad hoc responses to dislocation common in the United States.

The labor shortages characteristic of postwar Europe led many firms to hoard labor during economic downturns. The result is a two-pronged job protection strategy. Workers in viable firms are generally kept at work and partially compensated for working less than full time. In addition, some workers who would have been laid off are trained at government expense during slack periods. Workers displaced by firms not likely to survive are given advance notice of dismissal and an opportunity to participate in cooperative arrangements that favor early retirement, transfers to other plants, and relocation or retraining assistance. Since many dismissals must be justified publicly to labor courts or plant-level workers' councils, mass dismissal decisions, when they occur, are often more acceptable to affected workers.

Most U.S. special protection programs offer weekly payments as compensation for loss and leave the adjustment process up to the displaced worker. By contrast, European countries typically erect a much more elaborate web of protections. The need to justify mass dismissals keeps European workers in place longer. Once dismissed, public and private income maintenance systems replace 80 to 90 percent of a worker's lost earnings, a U.S. level attained only when collective bargaining agreements supplement regular UI and TAA.

European assistance does more than replace earnings. Almost all unemployed Europeans continue to be covered by national health care systems, whereas only one-third of America's unemployed have private medical insurance.[2] Most dismissed European workers have contributions made on their behalf to the social security system, limiting pension reductions due to lengthy unemployment spells. Extensive European regional and industrial policies are more likely to bring new jobs to high unemployment areas.

This chapter reviews the economic background which prompted the creation of postwar assistance programs in Europe. The second section describes worker protections available today. The final section assesses European job security programs.

The Economic Background, 1950–1980

Economic circumstances and job protections vary from country to country, but at least seven socio-economic factors play a larger role in most European countries than in the United States. First, most European governments are more interventionist than the U.S. government, willing to nationalize important economic sectors and prone to intervene and make private decisions sensitive to social consequences. Second, the memory of prewar government instabilities traceable to the 1930s depression makes full employment a higher priority than antiinflation efforts in most European countries. European nations have had consistently low unemployment rates in the postwar period, although most nations' unemployment rates increased to U.S. levels after 1979. Third, employment is subject to more regulation in Europe. Most countries require employers to negotiate lay-off and dismissal plans with both unions and independent plant-level workers' councils. Employer lay-off and dismissal plans can be appealed to special labor courts.

Individual employers are further constrained by the fourth and fifth factors, strong unions and employer associations. Except for France and Italy, most European wage and salary workers are organized into unions that often bargain with industry-wide employer associations. Individual employers are bound by the agreements reached whether they belong to the association or not. This collective labor-industry bargaining process promotes uniform wages and working conditions. If employment problems occur, they are usually throughout the industry.

Two final factors impact directly on economic dislocation, dependence on international trade and manpower policies. The need to export over such a long period has made most Europeans aware of the need to promote adjustment to efficiency-increasing changes. Labor adjustments are expedited by a variety of individual job protections and a tradition of tripartite cooperation to tackle economic and employment problems.

Three of the above factors were especially important for the evolution of job protection policies. First, peace-time rebuilding in an era of slowing population growth and rapid output expansion assured most European economies full employment and even labor shortages by 1960.[3] Second, a tradition of governmental intervention lent itself to the establishment and coordination of regional development policies, macro-economic investment programs, and labor market policies. The third influence on European decision making has been the need to export a significant fraction of GNP. Although intentions and results vary, it is generally true that export dependence promoted cost-cutting efficiency in industry, while interventionist governmental policies and strong trade unions guaranteed full employment.

The need to remain efficient despite tight labor markets has engendered both public and private job protection programs. The result is a variety of programs that provide far more protections and assistance for the typical European worker facing dismissal than his U.S. counterpart enjoys. Not surprisingly, European workers are usually more willing to accept displacement.

Europe's economic growth and comprehensive protection programs have minimized opposition to labor displacement for twenty-five years. However, the oil price hikes of 1973 and 1979 resulted in high unemployment, inflation, and the displacement that typically follows rapid change in international markets. The experiences of the past few years also highlight some of the disadvantages of the European system. For example, the existence of strong unions and employer associations encouraged reliance on tripartite committees to deal with most industrial and labor problems on an industry-wide basis. Now that job preservation has become as important as international efficiency, protectionist sentiment is industry-wide. Similarly, the tradition of bringing jobs to people has kept dismissed workers in depressed areas even when labor is needed in other places.

Job Protection Programs

European labor protection programs fall into two broad classes: programs covering temporary lay-offs and those dealing with permanent dismissal. Since some lay-offs turn into permanent dismissals and some dismissals prove to be only temporary lay-offs, there is some merging of the two in practice. In both instances, individual workers have administrative and legal rights before lay-off and, if unemployed, receive relatively generous compensation and maintenance of medical insurance and pension contributions.

Short-run lay-offs are discouraged in most European countries. In these countries, an employer must consult with a plant or factory-level workers' council before laying off employees. In some countries (France), the employer must secure lay-off approval from the Department of Labor. Although most employers wanting to make lay-offs eventually succeed, the net effect of these consultations and permission procedures is to delay lay-offs for several weeks to several months.

Laid-off workers are entitled to unemployment insurance in all European countries. Conditions of eligibility and the amount and duration of benefits vary between countries, but most unemployed Europeans are entitled to relatively higher benfits for longer periods than are their counterparts in the United States. For example, unemployed German workers receive 68 percent of their previous net monthly earnings for one year, and a means-tested 54 percent unemployment assistance indefinitely thereafter.[4] German workers getting UI benfits retain their health insurance, accumulate pension credits, and continue to receive UI credits that initiate benefits in the event of future lay-offs. The Swedish UI system, administered by the trade unions, offered an average (taxable) benefit of $200 weekly for up to 300 days (450 days for workers fifty-five and older) in 1979. New labor force entrants are entitled to $15 daily until they find a job. French UI benefits are 75 percent of an unemployed worker's previous salary and $9.00 daily for new labor force entrants and reentrants.

Instead of temporary lay-offs, several countries prefer to maintain workers at their jobs but on a shortened work week. These short-time workers put in twenty or thirty hours weekly, but are paid for almost full-time work by their employers, who are reimbursed from government funds.[5] In Germany, for example, workers can be kept on short work weeks up to two years, and about 2 to 4 percent of the work force is on a short work week at any given time (550,000 workers in March 1982, compared to 1.8 million unemployed). Generally, overtime work is severely restricted or banned when workers are on short-time. Employers must show that a shortened work week is unavoidable, temporary, and due to economic circumstances.

A German worker on short-time receives both earnings and a short-time payment, for example, if hours are reduced 10 percent, the worker gets 99 percent of his previous net earnings. As the work week gets shorter, the worker's net pay approaches the normal 68 percent UI benefits.

Instead of short-time work, some European labor leaders are demanding a thirty-five-hour work week to create more jobs. Heinz Vetter, president of Germany's Deutsche Gewerkschafts/Bund (DGB), argues that "the most important means of fighting unemployment remains the shortening of working times, with the thirty-five-hour week the general target to be aimed for."[6] IG Metall, Germany's largest union, is expected to make the thirty-five-hour work week a key demand in 1984 contract negotiations. Demands for a shorter work week are heard in Holland and in Britain, where 73 percent of all manual workers have agreements to cut the forty-hour work week to thirty-nine hours by the end of 1982.[7] Negotiations in France have produced a thirty-nine-hour week and a fifth week of paid vacation for most workers, although the (dominant) Communist and Socialist union federations want to cut the work week to thirty-five hours. The push for a shorter work week is not as pronounced in Scandinavia.

Some governments subsidize employers to maintain production and employment by paying up to 75 percent of wages for those workers slated for dismissal. Sweden, for example, encouraged firms planning dismissals in 1976-1977 to build up inventories. The program was finally abandoned when it became clear that the world-wide recession would be longer lasting than anticipated.

Public employment offices in Europe are generally considered much better at matching workers and jobs than the U.S. federal-state employment service. The Swedish Labor Market Board, for example, is a central clearing office for advance notice of lay-offs, apprenticeship and training programs, and subsidies for employers. Job vacancies are announced daily on state-owned radio and television networks, and Swedish newspapers carry the job vacancies which all employers must file with the Labor Market Board. Most European countries discourage private employment agencies, encouraging all jobs and applicants to be matched through the public employment service.

Permanent Dismissal

Permanent dismissal usually follows the same pattern of advance notice, unemployment insurance, and both training and relocation allowances.[8] Loss compensation, as in TAA and the railroad industry in the United States, is not the basis for worker protection programs in Europe. Because labor market policies are more comprehensive, displacements are anticipated and handled by agencies created to deal with dismissals.

The normal procedure for a company wanting to close all or part of a facility is to provide two to six months advance notice of its plans. In Germany and Sweden workers get their first inkling of planned dismissals from their representatives on a company's supervisory board of directors.[9] After high-level agreement on the need to dismiss workers, the company must consult with, and in some instances, negotiate an agreement regulating dismissals with the plant-level workers' council. In some basic industries (the German steel industry), the government and the workers' council have developed a comprehensive social plan to expedite the reemployment of displaced workers. Britain's 1975 Employment Protection Act requires all public and private employers to give two to three months notice to affected unions and the Department of Employment. Advance notice normally allows a company to begin reducing its work force through attrition and subsidized early retirement, but rarely do the parties notified succeed in reversing a company's decision to close a plant partially or totally.

Advance notice is usually given to the workers' council, the union, the government employment service, and the individual worker. The minimum notice required depends on the number and characteristics of workers involved. In Sweden, at least two months notice is required to dismiss up to twenty-five workers, but six months for more than one hundred. If workers forty-five and older or handicapped persons are to be dismissed, at least six months individual notice is required. French law requires at least one month's pay or one month's advance notice for all dismissed workers with at least six months' service and the approval of the Inspectorate of Labor. Since the Inspectorate can (and does) withold dismissal permission until workers find new jobs, French employers often try to find alternative jobs for redundant workers.

German law prohibits socially unjustified dismissal after a six months' probationary period of employment, and requires companies planning mass dismissals (defined as more than 25 percent of the work force for small employers and 10 percent or more for large employers) to give advance notice to the regional office of the Labor Department. German companies are also obliged to notify their plant-level workers' council and to negotiate the number and timing of dismissals and the assistance to be offered to displaced workers. The workers' council opinion on the need for dismissals must accompany the employer's advance notice petition to the regional labor office.

Advance notice is best suited to the production planning of large multi-plant firms. Smaller firms supplying large companies are often at their mercy. If a small auto supply firm is not informed of an impending auto assembly slow-down, it can find its market gone with less than six months notice. The requirement to pay workers' wages at least six months sometimes bankrupts smaller firms. Although advance notice to supplier companies has been discussed, no country yet requires one company to inform another of its production plans. Companies continue to rely on word-of-mouth to stay informed.

Few countries require severance pay for all dismissed workers. Britain's Redundancy Payments Act (1965) requires employers to pay dismissed workers who have had at least two years' service a minimum one and one-half weeks of severance pay for each year of employment with the firm. This lump-sum severance pay does not reduce a worker's normal UI benefit. Employers who dismiss workers according to statutory procedures recover 41 percent of total severance pay from the national unemployment insurance fund.

British unions can and do negotiate additional severance pay. The British Steel Corporation made $17,000 to $35,000 lump-sum payments to workers dismissed when it closed its Corby (England) steel mill.[10] In addition, the local housing authority reduced rents in public housing by 60 percent for unemployed workers. A joint European Economic Community (EEC)-British government fund either brings a displaced worker's wage up to 90 percent of its former level or seventy-eight weeks if he takes a lower paying job or continues to pay a displaced worker his full wage for one year if he enrolls in an approved training program. In most other European countries, severance pay is fixed by negotiation and is subject to appeal to labor courts. Belgium is generally acknowledged to have the highest severance pay—it can cost $250,000 to dismiss a worker.

Advance notice is usually coupled with the duty to justify dismissals. One response to advance notice of mass dismissals is a strategy of delay. If workers' councils, unions, government, or individual workers disagree with the dismissal decision, they can appeal the employer's decision to labor department offices and labor courts empowered to delay actual dismissals. These courts can order that dismissals be delayed and that the firm retain its workers by paying short work-week benefits, or getting government aid to subsidize inventory accumulation.

The need to justify dismissals usually means that the affected workers and unions at least grudgingly accept the final decision. The time that elapses until justification is secured permits a variety of targeted public and private assistance efforts to be offered to workers displaced and persuades employers to provide additional assistance in order to discourage time-consuming appeals.

The advance notice requirement and appeal options give workers facing dismissal a limited job property right that employers are willing to buy out with severance pay to induce quits. Employers sometimes induce voluntary quits by offering golden handshakes or severance pay. Volkswagen, partially state-owned, announced plans to dismiss 25,000 workers in one area in 1974. Opposition to the dismissals prompted a golden handshake program that offered up to $12,000 each to voluntary quitters, a scheme intended to appeal to women and foreign workers (who left the country after quitting). The Ford and Opel plans to trim their work forces 10 percent in 1979–1980 were estimated to cost at least $15,000 per voluntary quit. A 1981 agreement in the German cigarette industry encouraged early retirements by giving workers aged sixty-three or older the choice of 75 percent of their earnings for not working, or full wages for working twenty hours weekly (older workers could also work forty hours for full pay). Even with these ostensibly generous bribes to quit, some German students of displacement protections believe current laws and rules fail to protect workers.[11]

Workers receiving severance pay also get regular UI benefits. These UI benefits usually replace a higher fraction of an unemployed person's previous take-home wages for a longer period than is the case in the United States. U.S. UI benefits replaced an average 50 percent of gross earnings in 1975; most European countries replace more than 60 percent of previous net earnings. Further, the real value of European UI benefits is increased by the continuation of health insurance and pension contributions.[12] European UI benefits normally continue for at least one year, after which still-unemployed workers are eligible for means-tested unemployment assistance.

European countries operate extensive and expensive active manpower programs. Sweden spends almost 10 percent of its national budget—$2 billion annually—to train and retrain workers (a roughly equivalent U.S. expenditure would be $50 to $60 billion instead of the $8 billion spent through the Comprehensive Employment and Training Act (CETA) in 1981). Germany spends $1.5 to $2 billion annually for retraining and encourages participation by supplementing normal UI benefits to bring the earnings of training program participants up to 90 percent of their previous net earnings.[13] Thus, displaced workers have superior protection on three fronts:

1. Advance notice requirements and appeal options that encourage employers to bribe them to quit voluntarily.
2. Relatively generous regular UI benefits that also include maintenance of health insurance and pension coverage.
3. Eligibility for training and retraining in readily available government programs with monetary encouragement to participate.

Displaced workers may find jobs with new or expanding employers who have been induced to create jobs by industrial and regional policies. The tripartite Swedish Labor Market Board (AMS) coordinates labor and industrial policies, permitting a single agency to weigh trade-offs between dismissal and a variety of investment and employment subsidies, on-the-shelf needed public works projects, and training coordinated with the needs of employers. German industrial and regional policies do not permit Swedish fine-tuning but do subsidize investments in specific areas. Most European countries try to coordinate labor and regional policies.

European countries spend relatively more on industrial and labor policies than does the United States.[14] Most European countries believe their extensive programs are successful, even though none have made any significant effort to apply detailed cost-benefit analysis to them.[15] A general fear of unemployment and a tradition of cooperation between business, labor, and government portend continuation of the current mix of labor and industrial policies.

The fact that both workers and employers are relatively well-organized expedites industry-wide adjustments to change. If an industry faces structural adjustments (for example, autos or steel), the machinery to work out an adjustment program is already in place. Legislation that permits government to extend agreements to all firms in the industry encourages firms to compromise.

In sum, most European employers are encouraged to avoid dismissals. Before putting workers on temporary lay-off, employers may:

1. put workers on short work weeks, paying them for twenty to thirty hours of work and having government pay the balance of the weekly wage;
2. build up inventories that are carried with low-interest government loans and/or accelerate the delivery of government purchases;
3. receive grants to train and retrain workers in a plant during low production times.

If employers want to dismiss workers, they must first notify the affected union, the plant-level works council, the government, and the individual worker. Any of the four notified parties can find the justification inadequate and delay actual dismissals.

Most employers wanting to dismiss workers eventually succeed. Dismissed European workers:

1. often receive severance pay that varies with length of service but is often in the $10,000 to $20,000 range;
2. generally have a higher proportion of their after-tax earnings replaced for a longer period by the regular UI system than do U.S. workers;
3. usually retain health insurance coverage and often find their employer or the government continuing to make (high) pension contributions;
4. are eligible to participate in extensive retraining programs and/or obtain relocation assistance;
5. may find local work if other employers move to the area to take advantage of the investment, tax, and training subsidies offered through industrial and regional policies.

There are no European-wide rules that standardize job protections, but the European Economic Community (EEC) does maintain a special fund to compensate workers dismissed from coal and steel jobs. The EEC funds help displaced workers readapt by supplementing cash assistance payments and providing relocation and retraining aid. EEC coal and steel aid varies by country and age of the dismissed worker, for example, in 1979 the average EEC payment to a British worker was 930 pounds ($2,232).[16] EEC payments may continue for up to two and one-half years.

Pending EEC legislation would standardize job protection legislation. An EEC redundancy directive requires employers to give advance notice of dismissal to individual workers, unions, and labor department offices. It also requires justification and negotiation over planned dismissals and sets minimum standards for severance pay. It should be noted that most northern European job protection programs already exceed these minimum EEC standards. Severance pay requirements are collected from the parent company if a country's branch plants are closed. The American Badger Company (MA) closed its Badger Belgium subsidiary and left only the subsidiary's assets to cover severance payments. European courts ruled that the U.S. parent had to provide eight more months' severance pay for each worker.

Investment subsidies to create new jobs may be standardized also. Ford's 1979 auction of an auto plant and its 4,000 jobs to the countries offering the fattest subsidies (Britain and Spain) prompted the European Commission to request that all countries offer similar job-creation subsidies to avoid competitions that only increase company profits.[17] The Organization for Economic and Cooperative Development (OECD) urged its members (including the United

States) to adopt positive adjustment policies that phase out inefficient firms and aid individuals, not subsidize companies to preserve jobs.

Despite comprehensive assistance programs, the need to reduce employment in basic industries, especially steel, autos, textiles, and mining, has prompted special adjustment assistance programs. The French government took over two money-losing steel companies in 1979 (Usinor and Sacilor) and bought out 20,000 redundant workers with early retirements and severance pay. Displaced workers fifty-five or older get 80 to 90 percent of salary for one year and 70 percent per year thereafter; younger workers get a $12,000 severance payment. Workers are offered new local jobs and have the right to reject the first two offers without losing benefits.[18] The fact that the state has an ownership stake in many troubled French industries promises new pressures for these special displacement programs.

Will European governments continue adding SPPs and create two-tiered UI systems like the United States? No general trend is yet discernible. Henk Uredeling, the EEC Commissioner for employment and social affairs in 1980, proposed an EEC-wide rule that would require companies with fifty or more employees to prepare an annual report for workers that informed them of any company plans that might affect their employment. Some observers fear that if the EEC does not establish European-wide standards, (partial) government ownership may force individual firms to offer special adjustment assistance, especially if large numbers of workers face dismissal and dim prospects for recall. If so, then even mandatory advance notice, negotiation, and generous UI cannot overcome entrenched job property rights.

Canadian job protections parallel those in Europe. The Canadian Manpower Consultative Service sends teams to communities experiencing or threatened with mass dismissals. Tripartite committees are created to help cope with dislocation. This low-cost joint consultation is supplemented with a $290 million, six-town pilot program that subsidizes job creation and encourages worker relocation. Among the subsidies available is a $1.68 hourly wage payment to employers hiring laid-off workers over forty-five. Laid-off workers fifty-four and older unable to find another job are eligible for full unemployment benefits until pensions are available at age sixty-five.

Consultation and subsidies are being reinforced with tougher labor laws. The Canada Labor Code, which covers the 10 percent of the work force employed in federally regulated industries (for example, banks and airlines) and sets the standard for most provincial labor codes, requires companies to offer at least five days severance pay after one year of employment and an additional two days pay for each additional year of service. Companies with more than fifty employees must provide at least four months advance notice of lay-offs.[19]

In Japan, worker protection from lay-offs during business cycle downturns is a function of place of employment. About one-third of Japan's work force is employed by large firms that promise lifetime employment. Small firms, often subcontractors for the larger firms, serve as work force shock absorbers by making their hiring and lay-off decisions contingent on their workloads, derived from orders placed by larger firms. The lifetime system threatened to unravel after the 1974 recession, so the Japanese government decided to subsidize large firms by paying one-half of normal wages for workers who would have been laid off if employers agreed to retrain them instead. If a majority of firms in a structurally depressed industry appeals for assistance, firms become eligible for innovation loans, and workers receive extended UI benefits and additional job search assistance. In 1980, thirty-nine industries were designated structurally depressed.[20]

Assessment

European job protections are more comprehensive than those available to the typical U.S. worker. Tripartite economic planning, a commitment to full employment, active trade unions, plant-level workers' councils, and a history of exposure to the dislocations transmitted via international trade have made programs to assist displaced workers an integral part of European economic policies.

Most European economies had labor shortages between 1960 and 1973, expediting reemployment for anyone displaced. Today displacement is minimized because firms have to justify lay-offs and dismissals to their own board of directors (including worker representatives in Germany and Sweden), to plant-level workers' councils, and ultimately to labor courts. Instead of dismissal, many governments attempt to keep workers at work for twenty to thirty hours weekly and pay partial wages for the nonworked hours. Some governments avoid lay-offs by subsidizing inventory build-up, stepping up government purchases, or starting public works projects held in reserve.

European workers who are dismissed usually have at least two-thirds of their after-tax earnings replaced, have their health coverage extended and their pension contributions continued, and often receive severance pay. Most European countries operate extensive retraining programs and many subsidize worker relocation. Employment policies are linked to regional and industrial policies that encourage firms to create new jobs in depressed areas with investment and training subsidies.

The European job protection system worked remarkably well so long as unemployment was minimal and some fraction of lay-offs were absorbed by foreign workers returning home.[21] Since 1974, unemployment is higher and the alien guestworkers are no longer willing to return (and be denied reentry). Some employers want to emulate U.S. lay-off policies, arguing that dismissal must be an employer right, not a privilege granted by labor courts.[22] Furthermore, they argue that subsidized housing in depressed areas and housing shortages in regions with jobs make redundant workers reluctant to move. Subsidizing the entry of firms into depressed areas is too expensive. One British critic argues that the delays and rigidities of European job security systems that promoted labor peace in the past now mean that "governments for the most part have engaged in adjustment-resistance policies . . . rather than . . . adjustment-assistance policies."[23]

European economies now confront severe and persistent unemployment problems. This joblessness may persist because many of the experienced unemployed worked in the shrinking steel, chemicals, textiles, and shipbuilding sectors. Even after economic recovery, many experienced unemployed workers will not be recalled to their old jobs. However, European workers are reluctant to move to areas with expanding industries because of their sense of community, housing shortages, and generous unemployment benefits that do not require mobility. If job security and mobility systems are not revised, the duration of unemployment in Europe is likely to lengthen. For example, in France and the United Kingdom, about half the jobless were unemployed six months or more in October 1981.

The International Labor Organization (ILO) has joined the discussion on the side of those who argue that more flexibility and "anticipatory adjustment assistance" must replace "widespread adjustment resistance."[24] The ILO finds that the constitutional right to work and the difficulty of securing dismissals encourages employers to retain redundant workers. However, the ILO is expected in June 1982 to endorse a proposal that companies closing plants consult with affected workers. Job security is even more important in Eastern Europe. The ILO estimates that only 10 to 20 percent of all Soviet workers displaced by technological change are actually separated from their jobs.[25] To the extent that worker displacement results from Third World imports, some European countries propose a linking of free trade and fair employment standards.[26]

Developing countries realize that positive adjustment policies in industrialized nations can promote the adjustment of dislocated workers and stave off pressures for protectionism.[27] One former trade negotiator argues that continuous efforts to liberalize trade in the United States are necessary or else impacted firms and workers are likely to succeed in imposing further restraints on trade. On these grounds "TAA could be considered a foreign assistance program because, by promoting freer trade, it facilitates a transfer of resources to the developing countries."[28]

High unemployment, on the other hand, demands attention before it wreaks irreparable damage on Europe's social and political fabric.[29] The 10 million unemployed Europeans in a work force of 110 million mean Europe is experiencing its highest (9 percent) postwar unemployment rate. The worrisome upward trend in youth unemployment is prompting more calls for reduced hours, work sharing, on-the-job training, and inventory accumulation to create jobs. However, employers complain that more labor market interventions will undermine their competitiveness in international markets.

Notes

1. Douglas Fraser, quoted in *Economic Dislocation: Plant Closings, Plant Conversion* (Washington: UAW, USW, IAM, 1979), p. 2.

2. Ibid., p. 8.

3. Charles Kindleberger, *Europe's Postwar Growth: The Role of Labor Supply* (Cambridge: Harvard University Press, 1967), chapters 1-2.

4. To save money, a proposal was discussed to reduce the German UI benefit to 63 percent of a worker's previous net pay. The proposal was rejected for FY 1982. About 93 percent of Germany's work force receives an annual bonus that averages one month's wages.

5. British and German workers on short-time receive 75 percent of pay for time not worked.

6. Heinz Vetter, *Gleichberechtigung oder Klassenkampf-Gewerkschafts politik für die 80er Jahre* (Dusseldorf: DGB, 1980), p. 24.

7. "Europe's Unions," *The Economist,* September 5, 1981, p. 79.

8. Disabled workers are declared unfit to work and receive disability payments instead of UI. When unemployment is rising, definitions of disability prove very elastic. In the Netherlands, the disabled outnumber the unemployed two to one. Kees Bartels, Personal communication, September 9, 1981.

9. German *Mitbestimmung* or codetermination law operates on several levels. The 1951 law requires equal labor and management representation in iron, steel, and mining companies, with a neutral appointee holding the tie-breaking vote. The 1976 law covering all other companies with more than 2,000 employees (about 500 German firms) requires an equal number of worker and management representatives but gives the tie-breaking vote to a management appointee. The 1980–1981 Mannesmann controversy arose when Mannesmann merged its shrunken steel operations into its dominant pipe division and claimed that it is now covered by the 1976 law instead of the 1951 law. A January 1981 compromise may set a pattern for future mergers in the labor-displacing steel and mining sectors—Mannesmann will come under the 1976 law after a six-year wait.

10. Eric Morgenthaler, "When British Close Mills, the Government Gives an Array of Help," *Wall Street Journal,* September 24, 1980, p. 1. These large severance payments led some British advisers to predict that unemployed steel workers would reopen some of the small businesses that went bankrupt.

11. F. Boehle and B. Lutz, *Rationalisierungsschutzabkommen* (Goettingen: Verlag Otto Schwartz, 1974).

12. However, the United States has more two-earner families because women's labor force participation rates are higher in the United States than in most European countries.

13. In 1980, the German Labor Office spent DM 21.7 billion—DM 8.1 billion for regular UI benefits, 1.5 billion for extended benefits, and the balance for training.

14. Several developing countries have even more extensive job protections despite widespread unemployment and underemployment. In Portugal, for example, workers cannot be fired. Proposals that would permit employers to fire workers for incompetence, alcholism, or chronic absenteeism still require that the job vacated by a firing be refilled. *The Economist*, October 24, 1981, p. 76.

15. C. Killingsworth, "Manpower Evaluations: Vulnerable but Useful," *Monthly Labor Review*, April 1975, p. 50.

16. *The Economist*, February 23, 1980, p. 60.

17. "Plant Subsidies in Europe Tightening," *New York Times*, February 18, 1980, p. D4.

18. "French Steel," *The Economist*, July 21, 1979, p. 78.

19. "Help for Recession-Battered Towns," *World Business Weekly*, February 16, 1981, p. 48.

20. Gary Saxonhouse, "Industrial Restructuring in Japan," *Journal of Japanese Studies*, 5(1979):273–320.

21. Even Japan's fabled lifetime employment system was strained by the 1973-1974 recession. Workers employed by the largest companies, about one-third of the total work force, expect their employers to keep them on the payroll until they are between fifty-five and sixty. When recession reduces an employer's need for workers and the work week is cut to spread the work, older workers are encouraged to retire earlier, and some workers are lent to other firms and industries. These often unwritten job security agreements are sometimes violated. The ship-building industry reduced employment by 111,000 between 1974 and 1979 by encouraging voluntary retirements and laying off a few workers.

22. A recent OECD study notes that some French employers "make increasing use of fixed-term appointments . . . to circumvent the restrictive legislation on dismissals." *Manpower and Employment Measures for Positive Adjustment* (Paris: OECD, 1979). p. 21.

23. Hugh Corbett quoted in Laura Wallace, "Protectionist Pressures are Rising in Europe as Economies Stagnate," *Wall Street Journal*, January 30, 1981, p. 1.

24. *Growth, Productivity and Employment in Europe* (Geneva, ILO, 1979) as summarized in *ILO Information*, October 1979, p. 6.

25. Ibid., p. 6.

26. Gus Edgren, "Fair Labor Standards and Trade Liberalization," *International Labour Review*, October 1979, vol. 118 no. 5, pp. 558–614.

27. *Implications for Developing Countries of the New Protectionism in Developed Countries* (Geneva: UNCTAD Secretariat, 1979).

28. Michael Aho and Thomas Bayard, "American TAA After Five Years," *The World Economy*, November 1980, p. 365.

29. Cited in "The Specter of Rising Unemployment," *World Business Weekly*, February 16, 1981, p. 32.

6 Reform Issues

Change and labor displacement are the prices we pay for a dynamic economy. Past economic growth suggests that, on balance, they are prices worth paying. The issue is how the benefits and burdens of change and displacement should be shared. Specific issues include the role of the federal government in erecting rules to govern the overall pace of change and the federal government's responsibilities for displaced workers.

Unemployment and labor displacement are interdependent economic issues. The federal government can influence the pace of displacing change by regulating lay-offs. Alternatively, it can preserve jobs by subsidizing employers. Another strategy is to let employers make lay-off and dismissal decisions independently, and then assist unemployed workers. If the assistance after displacement option is selected, government can either maintain a single UI system or it can supplement basic UI benefits for selected displaced workers.

Few reformers believe the federal government should adopt general policies to slow the pace of changes that promote economic efficiency. Instead, most reforms propose improved programs to mitigate the hardships of involuntary labor displacement. The federal government has been searching for its proper role in displacement situations for at least two decades. Most people agree that "federal policies should indeed cushion the blow when sharp external shocks force an industry, its workers, and the communities within which it is located to undergo massive change in a short period of time."[1] The issue is how to provide this federal assistance.

This study recommends that the UI system be improved to provide benefits to laid-off workers for at least twenty-six weeks in each state. During this initial twenty-six-week eligibility, a worker should not be required to take an unsuitable job, to retrain, or to relocate. After twenty-six weeks, unemployed workers who have a low probability of being recalled to their old jobs should be encouraged to retrain or relocate. Workers accepting $200 to $1,000 relocation and retraining grants would remain eligible for UI benefits another twenty-six weeks. Workers who continue to wait for recall would have their benefits run out after another thirteen weeks.[2]

Most of the existing SPPs have sunset clauses. The transportation SPPs should be revised to stress relocation and retraining instead of wage maintenance. The open-ended and special loss programs should be phased out and affected workers assisted by an improved UI system. The disaster programs and consideration

93

clauses should be maintained. New SPPs should not be initiated to cope with labor displacement traceable to government actions or policies.

Instead of new SPPs, employers should be required to give six months or one year's advance notice if they intend to lay off a significant fraction of their work force (10 percent or more). Mandatory advance notice gives workers, employers, unions, communities, and the employment service time to plan for adjustments. Employers may find that workers, unions, and communities will make concessions to retain jobs or cooperate to increase efficiency and profitability.

Many unemployed workers are laid off only temporarily. Instead of releasing some workers and keeping the rest at work full time, employers should be encouraged to keep more workers at work by temporarily reducing the work week from five to four days. This work sharing means that workers do not have to readjust to their jobs after a period of unemployment and permits some workers who remain employed to be trained for new jobs. Workers would receive one-fifth of their normal UI benefit for the day they do not work.

Reforming Special Protection Programs

Federal concern for widespread labor displacement dates from the 1960s. The idea that the pace of technological change would displace prime-aged workers and impose special hardships on minorities and the unskilled prompted the formation of a National Commission on Technology, Automation, and Economic Progress. Charged with making recommendations to "facilitate occupational adjustment and geographical mobility" and to find ways to "share the costs and help prevent and alleviate the adverse impact of change on displaced workers," the Commission's 1966 report recommended macro-economic policies to assure full employment, public service employment (PSE) jobs for "those less able to compete in the labor market," and a negative income tax (NIT) or guaranteed annual income for those "who cannot or should not participate in the job economy."[3]

The 1966 recommendations were designed to treat all displacement equally, to permit the unemployed equal access to labor market information, a reformed employment service, relocation assistance, nationally uniform and improved unemployment insurance, and a safety-net role for PSE or NIT. Since there was no "good measure of the distress caused by displacement,"[4] the 1966 Commission recommended that general public measures to mitigate hardship be supplemented by private agreements worked out by labor and management.

Instead of general adjustment assistance programs, the federal government began to build on the relatively small special programs protecting specific groups of railroad workers from the adverse effects of change. Congress recognized that it had a special obligation to workers displaced because of federal actions that spread benefits across the nation. The number of special obligations it recognized increased rapidly in the 1970s. The result was the proliferation of SPPs. SPPs are under attack because they create a two-tiered UI system that cannot be justified by the cause or nature of the unemployment they mitigate.

SPP proliferation and rapidly increasing outlays have not satisfied beneficiaries, critics, or advocates of special displacement assistance. Beneficiaries complain of late, inadequate, or inequitable payments. Critics argue that payment of special loss compensation provides windfalls to selected workers and retards adaptation to necessary change. SPP advocates believe that even indirect government actions should not impose specific costs in order to generate widespread benefits.

Some of the dissatisfaction with SPPs arises from their unique position in the nation's income security system. SPP benefits are theoretically loss compensation, a payment for skills or seniority with a specific firm whose value is reduced because of a federal action or policy. The problem is that this loss is very difficult to calculate, especially at the time the worker is dismissed and in need of benefits. A worker's economic losses depend on how long it takes to find a new job and the wages and working conditions of the new job. Since it is impossible to estimate such losses before a displaced worker actually gets another job, it is hard to make an accurate one-time loss compensation payment to help displaced workers reach retraining or relocation decisions. Because lump-sum loss compensation is so hard to pay, weekly SPP payments are inevitably linked to regular UI payments.

Federal special protection programs can be abolished, extended, or maintained at current levels. Each reform option has advantages and disadvantages.

Abolishing SPPs would eliminate the need to establish a class of deserving unemployed eligible for extra benefits and instead would funnel UI assistance through one system. The causal link is responsible for much of the dissatisfaction with SPPs. Must government actions be only a major cause of the displacement or the major cause? What about displacement caused by the inaction of government? Should SPPs be established if government fails to halt gradual changes such as environmental damage that ultimately stops production? What if government responsibility is one step removed from actual displacement, for example, publicly funded mechanization research at land-grant universities that yields labor-saving machines refined and sold by private business to farmers?

The fundamental question is how to link degree of culpability with special benefit payments. One could try to quantify public responsibility for displacement and pay that fraction of losses to displaced workers; if tariff reductions increased imports and caused 40 percent of worker losses, then compensate displaced workers for 40 percent of total income losses. Even if analysis could determine the government's share of displacement responsibility, it would be hard to make payments because losses are not distributed equally among affected workers, requiring a second estimate of the public share of each worker's loss.

Alternatively, a uniform benefit schedule could assist affected workers if government was the major cause of displacement. The problem with this currently used test is that any line separating eligibles and noneligibles is arbitrary—if government must be at least one-third responsible, is it equitable to deny benefits to workers only 32 percent affected but grant them to 34-percent impacted workers?

SPP systems could go further, compensating displaced workers for the amount of loss or linking compensation to public benefits. Older workers in high-wage industries would receive proportionately more benefits than younger and lower-paid workers. Making benefits a fraction of the previous wage is one way to link payments to specific losses. Linking compensation to public benefits is difficult because many of the change-wrought benefits like redwoods preservation are hard to quantify. Most changes result in continuous future benefits (such as lower prices with imports). How should these future benefits be discounted to assess their current worth?

An unemployed individual's true losses cannot be known until a displaced worker finds another job and knows his new lifetime earnings stream. Since it is impossible to calculate real losses at the time of displacement, most SPPs pay (easily stopped) weekly benefits instead of making lump-sum compensation payments. But each SPP establishes its own eligibility criteria and offers a unique mix of benefits. The result is a time-consuming certification procedure and an explicit link with other income security programs, since most SPP programs reduce benefits if, for example, UI payments are also being received.

Individual certification and easily stopped weekly payments are attempts to limit windfall payments and to curb work disincentives. But even a perfectly functioning certification and payment system could not avoid making payments to those who would have quit anyway. Certification also denies benefits to workers who would have entered the industry had not government actions eliminated jobs.

Most SPP programs involve supplemental cash payments. But the job-training and relocation services provided by SPPs are also subject to criticism. These programs are too small in relation to cash benefit levels and not adapted to the special needs of experienced workers. The Department of Labor has responded to this criticism by proposing a pilot positive adjustment assistance program that would test alternative approaches to helping displaced workers. A Carter administration request for $50 million envisioned ten pilot projects in 1982, but was deleted from the Reagan FY 1982 budget.

The Reagan administration's proposals to limit UI and TAA payments promise to reduce outlays but will not reform the jobless-aid system. Surprisingly, some observers believe unions will not fight hard to retain TAA benefits, since TAA just didn't work, according to a clothing-workers'-union official.[5] If TAA only is a second best solution for the federal government and affected unions, a reformed UI program is a better option for all workers.

Should new SPPs be created to assist unemployed workers? Several proposed SPPs sought to limit the required link between government action and unemployment that normally justifies an SPP. A 1975 proposal endorsed by Congress but vetoed by President Ford would have amended the Public Works and Economic Development Act of 1965 to provide special benefits to workers unemployed because of antipollution activities. A Surface Mining Reclamation Act proposed in 1973 would have extended special benefits to workers unemployed as a result of the act. Similarly, the National Energy Emergency Act of 1973 (vetoed by President Nixon) would have provided benefits for up to two years to workers who had exhausted their UI benefits or were not eligible for regular UI. Causality was addressed at length in this bill. Assistance was to be provided "if such unemployment heretofore or hereafter is the result of the energy crises."[6]

If new SPPs are established, they must be less ambiguous than current legislation. The questions requiring answers include:

What unemployment will future SPPs cover; that traceable to federal actions, state and local policies, and/or other causes of unemployment?

How direct must the link be between government action and eligibility for SPP benefits?

Should SPPs certify eligibility individually or presumptively certify a group of workers for benefits?

Should SPP benefits vary with length-of-service or should all workers employed as of a certain date be eligible for the same benefits?

Should SPP benefits supplement UI or simply extend regular UI benefits to 52 or 104 weeks? How much should the SPP supplement be? Should the SPP supplement be available as a lump-sum payment too?

Should partial SPP benefits be available to workers partially displaced, for example, on reduced hours or bumped into lower paying jobs?

How should new SPPs be funded and administered?

Instead of expanding existing SPPs or beginning new ones, current SPPs could be phased out. This option appears most desirable. Most existing SPPs contain termination dates. Instead of terminating current SPPs before then, existing programs could be revised to stress relocation and retraining and new ones resisted.

Special Protection Programs and Unemployment Insurance

UI pays $15 to $20 billion to unemployed persons annually. SPP payments added over $3 billion to these UI payments in FY 1981. If SPPs continued to double their outlays annually, SPP payments would have exceeded UI benefits by 1986. However, President Reagan reduced SPP benefits sharply, to about $1 billion in FY 1982.

This study argues that the UI system should be reformed and SPPs phased out. Efficiency, equity, and administrative simplicity argue for a unified UI system. However, a single UI system does not require uniform benefits to all individuals. UI benefits can continue to be linked to an individual's employment and earnings record, thereby linking payments to earnings losses. If specific displaced workers are to be granted extra assistance, they could be permitted to draw regular UI benefits for longer periods of time. In addition, all unemployed workers should be eligible for subsidized retraining and relocation assistance.

What should a reformed UI system include? First, an individual's benefits should be 60 percent of his previous net earnings in every state. A 60 percent UI benefit corresponds to the recommendations of the 1980 National Commission on Unemployment Compensation (NCUC). The NCUC recommended a maximum UI benefit of 55 percent of a state's average weekly wage in 1982, rising to 60 percent in 1984 and 66.66 percent in 1986. The 60 percent standard increases the norm endorsed in 1973, when the UI goal was "to provide at least 4/5 of the Nation's insured workforce half-pay or better when unemployed."[7]

The primary objection to a national UI benefit standard is political. A federal standard would transform the current decentralized UI system, "into a system that is largely federalized."[8] Father Becker opposes a federal benefit standard for UI because of this threatened centralization and increased federal regulation, because of the problems inherent in selecting the average wage, and because of fears that abuse of the UI system by recipients may undermine support for a basic social institution.

These objections are not compelling. The main objection—increased federal control over a now decentralized system—is necessary if we are to eliminate one of the artificial incentives states use to attract and keep industries. Economic interdependence should encourage states to remove artificial incentives so that the United States can reap the true efficiencies of comparative advantage, not maintain or increase them. A national benefit standard that increases the maximum UI benefit automatically with a state's average wage—a procedure now followed by thirty-six states—would promote both efficiency in the allocation of resources and equity for laid-off workers. Furthermore, a uniform UI benefit formula would remove one of the current objections to termination of TAA, the fact that simply extending regular UI benefits to import-displaced workers will result in different payments to workers in neighboring states (up to $85 weekly in Missouri but $154 in Illinois). TAA has established a national UI benefits uniform nationally.

Basic eligibility standards should also be uniform. UI benefits should be available for at least twenty-six weeks in every state. UI recipients should be entitled to maintain their health coverage through their old employers, either at no cost or by having health care premiums deducted from UI benefit checks.

Most discharged workers will rightfully expect their lay-off period to be short. Since these workers have firm-specific skills and training, they should not be required to participate in retraining and relocation programs for the first twenty-six weeks of unemployment.[9] After twenty-six weeks, those still unemployed should be evaluated. If possible, this review should include both UI and CETA counselors.[10] If an unemployed worker is likely to be recalled, UI benefits should be available for an additional thirteen weeks. If not, an unemployed worker should be encouraged to retrain and/or relocate with small subsidies and the promise of an additional twenty-six weeks of UI benefits.

Workers forty-five and older should be eligible for the additional twenty-six weeks UI automatically. Even though the insurance principle mandates that all covered workers be eligible for the same earnings-linked benefits as soon as they work long enough to qualify, equity and reemployment experience dictate special consideration for older workers. The equity argument is simple. We already make distinctions between employers. Employers who are able to minimize lay-offs are rewarded with a lower UI tax. However, young workers with intermittent employment who qualify are eligible for the same UI benefits as older workers with history of continuous employment. In addition, the length of UI benefits is (or should be) related to the expected duration of unemployment, justifying, for example, extended benefits when unemployment is high. Older workers are likely to be unemployed longer than young persons after being laid off.

What would an improved UI system cost? In 1981, the average weekly UI benefit is expected to be $101, which replaces an average 36 percent of the $279 the average UI recipients' could be expected to earn. If the weekly benefit replaced 60 percent of the average recipient's wage, the direct additional costs would be $666.1 million weekly in 1981 or $7 to $8 billion annually. However, the total cost of increasing the average UI benefit to $167 from $101 weekly may be greater because higher UI benefits may discourage quick reemployment.

How much longer will the average spell of insured unemployment be if the average replacement benefit is 60 percent of average weekly earnings? No one knows. Hammermesh suggests that an increase in weekly UI benefits from 50 to 60 percent of the previous net weekly wage will prolong unemployment by half a week.[11] This response estimate is valid only for small changes in UI benefits. A 60 percent national standard will mean a nonmarginal benefit increase in many states. A lower bound estimate of the indirect cost of increasing weekly benefits is $505 million weekly (an extra $50 paid to 10.1 million UI recipients).

Critics of UI believe that current replacement ratios prolong unemployment. UI critics argue that lower UI payments and better labor market information could reduce the time required to lower an unemployed worker's reservation wage and thus reduce unemployment.

These UI critics believe in the virtues of elastic individuals able to respond quickly to changing prices. But an affluent society should not expect laid-off workers to immediately lower their expected wage—how could the individual's value of marginal product be halved overnight? We should expect longer job searches as general wage levels rise and as we provide earnings replacement insurance to cushion abrupt earnings losses. This income protection means that "the temporarily unemployed worker need not feel compelled by financial pressures to take a job below his normal skill and earnings level and thereby jeopardize or sacrifice the vocational progress he has made."[12] It should be remembered that the vast majority of unemployed workers do not draw benefits for their entire eligibility period and that many delay filing for benefits.

Furthermore, advocates of limited UI benefits are only arguing for a static saving. Limited UI benefits may deny the United States much larger dynamic gains. Inadequate assistance encourages resistance to change. The attempt to save a few UI dollars could wind up costing the economy far more in continued inefficient production. Instead of giving individuals incentives to stop or delay threatening economic change, we should provide overly generous transitional aid for displaced workers. Thurow argues that "what we lose in overly generous compensation, we will more than make up in faster economic change" that will increase productivity and output.[13]

Improved UI benefits, extended health insurance, retraining, and relocation assistance would provide a unified assistance program and obviate the need for additional special protection programs. This unified system would be more equitable to individuals, promote employer efficiency, and reduce current certification and administrative costs.

The call for a unified program to assist unemployed and displaced workers dates from the early 1960s, when SPPs were considered to be only transitional measures. Stanley Metzer, a chairman of the U.S. Tariff Commission, thought that "special adjustment assistance . . . may serve the purpose in time of raising the levels of adjustment assistance available generally, . . . (even though it is) difficult to justify differential treatment of adjustment problems on the basis of varying impersonal causes."[14] Metzer went on to note that workers have no more right to maintenance of tariff protection than do missile builders to maintaining their particular missile system.

The notion that all unemployed persons should be eligible for training and benefits was endorsed by a 1968 Task Force on Occupational Training in Industry. Nine of the sixteen Task Force members argued for a "guarantee of minimum levels of training to all Americans."[15] A 1972 review of federal adjustment assistance programs concluded that the categorial nature of SPP benefits "represents a failure to appreciate the fundamental commitment Congress has already made to the goals of skill adaptability and work-ethic acquisition."[16]

Increased UI benefits will help individuals. Revising the payroll tax system that now finances UI may discourage frequent lay-offs and end the subsidy stable employers now provide to unstable ones. One financing reform would have the payroll tax rise nonlinearly; if an employer laid off more than 5 percent of his work force each quarter, he could be subject to a greatly increased UI tax. Using the payroll tax as a penalty to prevent unemployment would emphasize

John Commons' view of UI's primary purpose.[17] This payroll tax reform could be coupled with a plan to provide UI funds to supplement the earnings of workers kept on employer payrolls on a part-time basis instead of being completly aid off.

Increasing UI payroll taxes for unstable employers will generate some of the additional revenue needed to finance a standardized UI system. Another source of funds is the taxes that now go uncollected when companies take advantage of state job promotion schemes. Forty-six states have some form of tax forgiveness or subsidy programs to attract new businesses. Although the various "state tax laws are so complex and diverse that no one has calculated the total revenue loss involved,"[18] states are believed to give up several hundred million dollars annually. However, these tax incentives seem to have very little effect on where companies decide to locate, so a nationwide abolition of tax exemptions would not affect any state's job growth.[19]

Advance Notice

A unified UI system can still be supplemented with features that protect workers from abrupt change. Instead of isolating publicly inspired changes for special treatment, a reformed system could cushion dislocations by requiring advance notice of all lay-offs and dismissals. Employers failing to give adequate advance notice would be required to provide severance pay. These public measures can still be complemented by private protection programs that deal with specific displacement situations.

Advance notice is the cheapest and often the most effective device to reduce displacement-caused earnings losses. Advance notice is a very common precondition for lay-offs in Europe and permanent dismissal under collective bargaining agreements in the United States.

Most U.S. employers resist mandatory advance notice. They want to avoid customer defections and minimize quits by the best and brightest workers who are first to leave and hard to replace. However, a survey of multiplant employers showed that most do provide advance notice and that few suffer productivity losses as a result.[20] This survey and the experience of Douglas Fraser on Chrysler's board of directors, where he pushed for the establishment of a five member committee to ease the impact of auto plant closings, suggests that many firms resist advance notice because of false convictions about its effects. Even if it is true that selective quits may (further) impair productivity, it should be remembered that the employer is planning to close (at least part of) a facility. Springing the closure decision on workers merely maintains employer profits or limits losses a few more months while increasing worker adjustment costs.[21]

Advance notice is sometimes resisted because "attention will tend to focus on preventing the redundancies rather than preparing to cope with them." It is true that "the collective combatting of redundancies" in class-conscious Britain may inhibit adaption to the idea of rendundancy.[22] However, this collective response may be as much a reflection of inadequate adjustment assistance as it is a predictable outcome of group responses to dislocating change. Older workers whose pay is tied to seniority wage schedules sometimes resist closures if given advance notice because they have the most to lose.

The impacts of advance notice depend on the worker protections available and the kinds of labor markets that match displaced workers to new jobs. Advance notice provides (paid) time for job search. The time is most likely to be used for successful job search if a country's labor markets are not segmented, if employers do not rank job applicants by their cost of training and put older workers, minorities, and women at the end of the queue, and if there is little age discrimination, seniority, pay, or age-linked health and pension contributions. If older workers are displaced into labor markets that limit mobility, they are likely to resist dismissal. Advance notice then becomes a device for protecting some workers in jobs at the expense of the unemployed trying to gain entrance to protected labor markets.

Existing studies do not permit generalization about the effects of mandatory advance notice. Advance notice does encourage workers to try and find new jobs. There are instances where displaced older workers must compete with younger workers for new jobs. If employers offer career-type positions, younger workers are likely to be favored by employers. If, on the other hand, available jobs offer few rewards for continued service, older workers are likely to get jobs but be just as dissatisfied as younger workers.

Advance notice of dismissal can inspire union concessions to preserve jobs. Adverse developments in steel, autos, and rubber encouraged some workers to forego or defer negotiated wage and cost-of-living increases to keep their jobs. Meat-packing workers agreed in 1980 to accept faster assembly line speeds to avoid plant closure.[23] In 1982 they accepted a four-year wage freeze for 40,000 union members in exchange for an 18-month moratorium on plant closings. Advance notice gives workers a chance to offer concessions and preserve their jobs. In 1982, unionized workers have been willing to make wage concessions in exchange for increased job security.

Two states—Maine and Wisconsin—require companies closing plants with 100 or more employees to pay dismissed workers one week's wages for each year worked (Maine).[24] They must also give sixty days advance notice (Wisconsin). Bills to require advance notice of plant closings are pending in twenty-one other states.

Most of these advance notice proposals would require employers to give one or two years notice if they intend to close a plant with 100 or more emlpoyees or reduce their work forces more than 50 percent. In addition, many of the proposals require severance pay equal to a week's wages for every year of service and maintenance of health insurance benefits for one year after the lay-offs occur. The Michigan proposal would also require a company make a payment equal to 15 percent of its annual payroll to a community development fund.[25] A 1982 California proposal, the Employment Stabilization Act, would have required one year's notice and a week's severance pay for each year of employment, but would have exempted small businesses from the notice and severance pay requirements.

Federal legislation that would require advance notice and worker assistance has been introduced in the last three Congresses. The bill with the most sponsors (fifty-nine), the National Employment Priorities Act of 1981 (H.R. 5040), would:

> require business concerns which undertake changes of operations to give notice to the Secretary of Labor, and to affected labor organizations, employees, and local governments; to require business concerns to provide assistance to employees who suffer an employment loss caused by changes of operations; to authorize the Secretary of Labor to provide assistance to such business concerns, and to such affected employees and local governments; and for other purposes.

Hearings were held in 1980, but there is little chance that federal or state advance notice or assistance requirements will be enacted in 1982. Business is so confident that no restrictions on plant closings will be enacted that the subject was not even listed with the 105 issues of concern to business before the 97th Congress.

Work Sharing

Short-time pay can reduce unemployment by shortening the work week for all workers or by having two workers share a single job. Some writers distinguish work sharing (shortening the work week to minimize lay-offs) from job sharing (converting a full-time job into two or more permanent part-time positions).[26] However, most observers use the generic work-sharing term for all such job-increasing plans. Work sharing is advocated as a means of limiting unemployment and accommodating the presumed "majority of American workers who are seeking to work less than 'full-time'."[27] This number is expected to rise with more multiple-earner households and more flexible retirement systems. Fred Best's recent book evaluates seventeen work-sharing policy options, including early retirement, mid-career educational leaves, reductions in the standard work week, and shifting the cost of some fringe benefits to government so that employers have fewer incentives to reduce employment in order to save the fixed costs of each worker's fringe benefits. Work sharing is discussed widely but seems most suited to clerical and certain service jobs.

California enacted a Work Sharing Unemployment Insurance (SUI) Program in 1978 to cope with the public sector lay-offs expected in the wake of Proposition 13. Under the California program, an employer with 100 employees who must reduce his work force by 20 percent cuts the work week from five to four days for all his employees and WSUI pays all the employees one-fifth of their regular weekly UI benefit (the maximum is $24 for the day not worked). All 100 workers continue working and drawing partial UI benefits for up to twenty weeks. Employers who participate in this voluntary program pay additional UI taxes. If the affected workers are represented by a union, the union must agree with the employer's decision to participate.

An interim evaluation reveals that participating employers wanted to retain valued workers, believed that work sharing instead of lay-offs improved morale, and discovered that work sharing reduced direct labor costs 21 percent versus only 16 percent for lay-offs.[28] Workers had their work time reduced an average 23 percent but their earnings were reduced only 7 percent. In general, the last hired, first fired workers vulnerable to lay-offs benefitted most by having their earnings maintained, while experienced workers whose seniority protected them from normal lay-offs got more leisure time.

Most of the participants in the California program are manufacturing firms with fewer than fifty employees. Since the program is voluntary, the positive experiences of the 1,300 firms and 40,000 workers participating should come as no surprise. Participating workers enjoy enhanced economic security because their continued job attachment increases earnings and maintains fringe benefits. However, organized labor is cautious about endorsing work sharing because of its potential threat to seniority rights. Participating firms like the enhanced worker morale, worker attachment, and the lower costs of work sharing UI, but business generally fears that WSUI may become a mandatory program that subsidizes marginal firms. The most enthusiastic proponents of work sharing are groups concerned about women and minority workers, because WSUI reduces lay-offs for these workers. Other states and Canada are experimenting with partial UI benefits for workers on short-time.[29] Representative Pat Schroeder introduced H.R. 3005 in 1981 to make partial UI benefits available to workers on short-time in all states.

Publicly mandated advance notice, short-time pay, and UI do not prevent workers from negotiating additional private protections. Employers and workers affected by displacement are best able to tailor local protections which are sensitive to specific displacement situations. Collective bargaining has shown itself to be a flexible instrument for dealing with labor displacement in many instances.

None of the reforms advocated here is a panacea.[30] Labor displacement will always be painful to workers and their communities. Improved UI benefits will not compensate for the psychological costs of job loss.[31] Change is necessary and inevitable, requiring significant costs and sacrifices. The challenge of job protection is similar to the other economic challenges we face. As Barry Bosworth notes, "The political problem is to shift the focus of public discussion away from the fruitless search for painless solutions to the question of how costs of the adjustments can be allocated in the most equitable way. The alternative of a continued drift in policy is becoming increasingly unpalatable and makes the ultimate solution more difficult."[32]

Summary

The federal government should continue to encourage efficiency-increasing changes. However, the system for assisting displaced workers must be reformed. Failure to reform the current system of SPPs and UI threatens to escalate costs and inequities. Simply limiting benefits may prove counterproductive if those threatened by change then resist it.

The special protection programs established by the federal government now add 25 percent to the nation's unemployment assistance bill. SPPs were created by Congress in recognition of a special obligation to workers and firms hurt by actions that spread benefits widely. In theory, SPPs compensate displaced workers for a loss of earnings caused by dismissal. However, it is not possible to calculate this earnings loss and make lump-sum payments that help displaced workers begin anew. Instead, SPPs pay easily stopped super UI benefits that simply compound work disincentives.

The best reform option is to phase out SPPs and channel all unemployment assistance through an improved UI system. Benefits that assure unemployed workers 60 percent of their previous wages promise the optimal trade-off between adequacy and work incentives. The special circumstances that surround lay-offs traceable to government actions should lengthen the period of eligibility for benefits and trigger special retraining and relocation assistance. Advance notice of dismissals should be mandatory to permit as many adjustments as possible before workers are unemployed.

The 1981–1982 rash of plant closings has heightened public sensitivity to one kind of labor displacement. Companies with plants scattered across the United States are closing their older and less efficient plants despite local protests. Businesses argue that they must have the flexibility to produce where costs are lowest; but some displaced workers and their communities believe that the current wave of plant shutdowns is an attempt to extract wage and regulatory concessions. The protest marches, petitions, and lawsuits engendered by plant shutdowns highlight the inadequacy of current public and private policies that assist unemployed workers and declining communities. To avoid no-win confrontations, the United States must develop positive adjustment policies that promote adaptation to change. Advance notice and UI reform are two positive adjustment policies.

The challenge of labor displacement will not fade away. The next two decades promise to make management more sensitive to capital costs and import competition. If business goes abroad to take advantage of docile labor, the workers remaining in the United States will be more vulnerable to displacement. The public policy challenge is to help these workers to move into expanding industries that can fully utilize their skills, not trap them in stagnant industries that argue for protection and subsidies.

Notes

1. *Economic Report of the President* (Washington: USGPO, 1981), p. 17.

2. This twenty-six week reexamination parallels the suggestions of the National Council on Employment Policy (Washington: Policy Statement of September 8, 1980). p. 16.

3. *Technology and the American Economy* (Washington: Government Printing Office, 1966), pp. 33-4.

4. Ibid., p. 20.

5. Quoted in the *Wall Street Journal's* "Labor Letter," February 24, 1981, p. 1.

6. Quoted in Rubin, "Proliferation," p. 798.

7. Quoted in Joseph Becker, *Unemployment Benefits: Should There Be A Compulsory Federal Standard* (Washington: American Enterprise Institute, 1980), p. 4.

8. Ibid., p. 54.

9. The Reagan administration must assume that most recent lay-offs are permanent dismissals. On February 25, 1981, Labor Secretary Donovan asked states to limit regular UI benefits to thirteen weeks beginning in October 1982. After thirteen weeks, workers could "be denied benefits if they refuse written offers of work which would pay wages at least as high as the minimum wage or their current UI benefits, whichever is higher."

10. *An Employment Strategy to Fight Recession and Inflation* (Washington: National Council on Employment Policy, 1980), p. 3.

11. Daniel Hammermesh, *Jobless Pay and the Economy* (Baltimore: John Hopkins, 1977), chapter 3.

12. Saul Blaustein, *Unemployment Insurance: Objections and Issues* (Kalamazoo: W.E. Upjohn, 1968), p. 7.

13. Lester Thurow, *The Zero-Sum Society* (New York: Basic Books, 1980), p. 210.

14. Stanley Metzer, *Trade Agreements and the Kennedy Round* (Fairfax, Va.: Coiner Publishers, 1964), pp. 55-6.

15. Task Force on Occupational Training in Industry, *A Government Commitment to Occupational Training in Industry,* 1967 President's Manpower Report to Congress, August 1968, p. 7.

16. Sidney Picker, "Adjustment Assistance for Employees: The Present Status of Federal Legislation," *Case Western Reserve Law Review* 23(1972):1569.

17. John Commons, "Unemployment Prevention," *American Labor Legislation Review* 12, April 1922. pp. 158-172.

18. John Herbers, "Survey Finds Tax Incentives Doing Little to Lure Businesses," *New York Times,* November 21, 1981, p. 1.

19. Ibid.

20. Arnold Weber and David Taylor, "Procedures for Employee Displacement: Advance Notice of Plant Shutdown," *Journal of Business* 36 (July 1963): 302-315.

21. D. Sease, "Closing of a Steel Mill Hits Workers in the U.S. with Little Warning," *Wall Street Journal*, September 23, 1980, p. 1. Workers were embittered by the closing of the Youngstown steel mill after they made work rule concessions to increase profitability and try to save their jobs.

22. W. Daniel, *Strategies for Displaced Employees* (London: PEP, 1970).

23. For details and additional examples see George Ruben, "Industrial Relations in 1980 Influenced by Inflation and Recession," *Monthly Labor Review,* January 1981, pp. 15-20.

24. Eight Maine poultry and shoe companies paid dismissed workers a total of $250,000 severance pay between 1977 and 1981. *Wall Street Journal,* September 29, 1981, p. 29.

25. The Michigan proposal is outlined by Ivar Peterson, "States Seeking Ways to Curb Impact of Closing Industrial Plants," *New York Times,* March 16, 1980, p. 26.

26. Noah Metz et al., *Sharing the Work* (Toronto: University of Toronto Press, 1981).

27. Fred Best, *Work Sharing: Issues, Policy Options, and Prospects* (Kalamazoo: Upjohn Institute, 1981).

28. Fred Best, Project Director, *The California Work Sharing UI Program* (Sacramento: Employment Development Department, 1981). WSUI savings exceed lay-off savings because the lower overall wages of the experienced and inexperienced workers who keep working more than offset higher fringe benefit costs.

29. The Canadian experience is discussed in Frank Reid, "UI-Assisted Worksharing as an Alternative to Layoffs: The Canadian Experience," *Industrial and Labor Relations Review,* April 1982, pp. 319-29.

30. Unanticipated policy shifts will still redistribute income. For example, the projected U.S. military build-up and social service cutbacks will raise the return to an engineering education and lower it for social work. Student selecting careers on the basis of the 1980 labor demands will enjoy windfall earnings gains or suffer unanticipated losses. Since students are not yet at work, even a reformed UI system could not account for sudden shifts in their earnings' prospects.

31. The psychological costs of job loss must be distinguished from workers' reactions to changing job content. A 1967 survey of U.S. workers whose jobs

were changed by new machine technologies found that "changes in job content and job characteristics associated with technological advance for the most part have favorable connotations." These job changes include increased job demands (job enlargement), reduced physical work effort, and greater opportunity to talk to fellow workers. Eva Mueller, *Technological Advance in our Expanding Economy* (Ann Arbor: Institute of Social Research, 1969), p. 14.

32. Barry Bosworth, "Economic Policy," in Joseph Pechman, ed., *Setting National Priorities: Agenda for the 1980s* (Washington: Brookings Institution, 1980), p. 70.

Appendix: Major Job-Protection Programs

Table A-1
Employee Protection Provisions Enacted into Federal Law

Title	Eligibility	Benefit amount	Duration	Other benefits	Administration	Funding source	Cost
1887							
Interstate Commerce Act, 49 USC 1(5) (2)(f) as amended in 1940. Also amended in 1976 to establish Rail Passenger Service Act (Amtrak) protections as minimum standards for railroad employee protection plans.	Any railroad employee affected by a transaction involving a railroad carrier or carriers, such as merger and consolidation.	Income protection option: Monthly income to equal former wages, reduced by any UI or income from other employment. Severance payment option: 3 months pay for 1–2 years service; 6 months pay for 2–3 years; 9 months for 3–5 years; 12 months for over 5 years.	Equal to the workers' length of service, up to a maximum of 6 years (4 years from 1940 through 1976).	(1) All relocation expenses. If employee is furloughed within 3 years of relocation and chooses to return to site of previous employment, railroad will pay all relocation expenses. (2) Fringe benefits preserved.	Interstate Commerce Commission.	Benefits funded by the railroads involved.	Not available.
1938							
Railroad Unemployment Insurance Act of 1938.	New employees: At least 5 months of employment and earnings of at least $1,000, with not more than $400 earned to be counted per month. Others: at least 3 months of employment and earnings of at least $1,000, with not more than $400 earned to be counted per month.	60 percent of daily wage rate up to $250 for 14-day period. Minimum of $12.70 per day.	Regular duration 26 weeks (130 compensable days). Extended duration for employees with 15 years service, 26 weeks; with 10–14 years, 13 weeks; with less than 10 years, 13 weeks only in periods of high unemployment (4 percent IUR). Benefits may not exceed base year wages.	(1) Cash sickness benefits (including maternity benefits).	Railroad Retirement Board.	Payroll tax on railroad employers.	Approximately $4.14 billion from 1939 to June 1979 (includes both unemployment and sickness benefits).

Law	Employees covered	Wage/protection provisions	Time period	Benefits	Administration	Carriers/bodies involved	Cost
1943 Federal Communications Act amendments of 1943 (Public Law 78-4) 47 USC, sec. 222 (f).	Any employee earning less than $5,000 per year affected by consolidation or merger of communications carriers.	Individuals whose employment began on or before Mar. 1, 1941, receive 100 percent wage protection, including fringe benefits. Individuals whose employment began after Mar. 1, 1941, discharged within 4 years of merger approval receive severance pay at 4 weeks pay per year of continuous service.	4 years	(1) Moving and relocation allowances for transferred employees. (2) Preference in hiring. (3) Maintenance of pension, health, and insurance benefits.	National Labor Relations Board responsible for enforcement of provisions to be implemented by communications carriers.	Communications carriers involved.	Not known.
1964 Urban Mass Transportation Act of 1964 (Public Law 88-365) 49 USC sec. 1609.	Any employee affected by Federal UMTA grants to a public body to improve mass transportation.	Provisions identical to IC Act of 1887, as amended.	Provisions identical to IC Act of 1887, as amended.	(1) Paid training and retraining. (2) Reemployment priority. (3) Continuation of collective bargaining rights. (4) Preservation of rights and benefits under existing bargaining agreements.	Secretary of Labor certifies employee protection provisions, administered by the bodies receiving UMTA grants.	Public bodies receiving UMTA grants.	No substantial cost.

Table A-1. Continued

Title	Eligibility	Benefit amount	Duration	Other benefits	Administration	Funding source	Cost
1965							
Public Works Economic Development Act, 42 USCA sec. 3243 (benefit provisions added by Public Law 93–423 in 1974), expired **Sept.** 30, 1979, but is pending renewal.	Individuals employed in area determined by Secretary of Commerce as experiencing (or threatened by) rise in unemployment or other economic problems or an area that has demonstrated long-term economic deterioration.	Up to maximum UI benefit payable in State. Reduced by any UI received.	Maximum duration of 1 year after unemployment begins.	Relocation expenses including travel and living expenses plus compensation for loss of selling house (or an amount equal to closing costs) plus payments for loss due to cancellations of lease.	Grants by Secretary of Commerce transferred to Department of Labor.	Congressional appropriation.	No money expended as yet.
High Speed Ground Transportation Act of 1965 (Public Law 89–220), 219 U.S.C. 1631.	Any employee of an entity receiving DOT grants to research and assist development of high-speed trains, who is directly affected by such grants; i.e., whose worsening of position can be shown to be a direct result of such grants.	Same as UMTA of 1964.	Same as UMTA of 1964.	Same as UMTA of 1964.	Secretary of Transportation must specify terms and conditions of employee protection as determined by the Secretary of Labor to be administered by the grantees.	Entities receiving DOL grants.	No substantial cost.
1966							
Demonstration Cities and Metropolitan Development Act of 1966 (Public Law 89–754). Employee protection provisions added by amendment of National Mass Transportation Assistance Act of 1974.	Any employee affected by transportation-related programs funded by the act.	Same as UMTA of 1964.	Same as UMTA of 1964.	Same as UMTA of 1964.	Same as UMTA 1964.	Entity receiving grants.	No substantial costs.

1970

Rail Passenger Service Act of 1970 (Amtrak) Public Law 91–518, 45 USC 501 et seq.

Employees adversely affected by National Rail Passenger Service's (Amtrak) takeover of intercity rail operations.

Up to 72 months.

Income protection option: Monthly income to equal former wages reduced by any UI or income from other employment. Fringe benefits also preserved. Severance payment option: 3 months pay for 1–2 years; 5 months pay for 2–3 years; 9 months pay for 3–5 years; 12 months pay for over 5 years.

(1) Training and retraining.
(2) Reemployment priority.
(3) Preservation of collective bargaining rights and benefits.

Railroad involved.

Railroads absorbed by National Rail Passenger Corp. responsible for absorbing cost.

Records not readily available.

1973

Regional Rail Reorganization Act of 1973, 45 USCA sec. 771 (Public Law 93–236) (Conrail) indefinite.

Workers adversely affected because of railroad reorganization.

Until age 65 for workers with 5 or more years service; period equal to prior service for those with fewer than 5 years.

100 percent of average pay for prior 12 months. Reduced by any UI or railroad earnings and by 50 percent of any other earnings. Separation allowance up to $20,000 depending upon years of service, age, position.

Relocation expenses including travel and living expenses plus compensation for loss in selling home (or an amount equal to closing cost), plus loss due to cancellation of lease.

Railroad Retirement Board reimburses carriers for benefits.

$250 million appropriated by Congress into Northeast Rail Transportation Protective Account.

$248 million by January 1980.

Table A-1. Continued

Title	Eligibility	Benefit amount	Duration	Other benefits	Administration	Funding source	Cost
Federal-Aid Highway Act of 1973 (Public Law 93–87) 23 U.S.C. 101 et seq.	Employee affected by urban mass transportation projects supported by Highway Trust Fund and Interstate Transfer moneys.	Same as UMTA of 1964.	Same as UMTA of 1964.	Mass transportation entity involved, under guidelines as approved by Secretary of Labor.	Mass transportation entity involved.	Entity involved.	No substantial cost.
1974							
Trade Act of 1974 (Public Law 93–610) (supersedes Trade Expansion Act of 1962) through Sept. 30, 1982.	Workers certified as adversely affected by increase in imports and either laid off or on 80 percent or less of average weekly wage and hours. Qualifying work: 26 of 52 weeks in adversely affected work at wages of at least $30 per week.	70 percent of worker's average weekly wage with maximum equal to national average weekly manufacturing wage (currently $250). Reduced by any UI received and by 50 percent of any wages received.	Maximum of 52 weeks in a 2-year period or, if worker is over 60 or in training, 78 weeks in a 3-year period.	Relocation allowances (80 percent of moving expenses plus maximum $500 lump sum), training (allowances plus travel and subsistence expenses), job search (80 percent of transportation and living expenses up to $500 while looking for work).	Through State unemployment insurance offices.	Federal general revenues through congressional appropriations.	$706,708,488 April 1975–April 1979.
Disaster Relief Act of 1974 (Public Law 93–200).	Workers unemployed as direct result of major disaster declared by President at request of Governor.	Act authorizes President to provide appropriate payment. Regulations provide weekly benefit equal to UI individual would have received if all wages were covered. Reduced by any UI or wages received.	Maximum duration of 1 year beginning with date disaster is declared.	Relocation expenses plus grants (up to $5,000) for necessary expenses plus rental or mortgage payments up to 1 year, plus cost of minor home repair.	State unemployment offices for cash benefits, Department of Agriculture for Food Stamps, HUD.	Appropriated as required annually by Congress.	$95,480,841 (through May 1979).
Juvenile Justice and Delinquency Prevention Act of 1974 (Public Law 93–415).	Employees affected by deinstitutionalization of juvenile delinquents.	Same as UMTA of 1964.	Same as UMTA of 1964.	Same as UMTA of 1964.	Law Enforcement Assistance Administration approves employee protection plans of institutions involved.	Institutions involved through Federal grant formulas.	No substantial cost.

1975					
Developmental Disabilities Services and Facilities Construction Act of 1975 (Public Law 95–103). Superseded by Developmentally Disabled Assistance and Bill of Rights Act, Public Law 95–602.	Employee who is affected by deinstitutionalization of the developmentally disabled.	No cash benefits.	Not specified.	(1) If dismissed State or local government employee cannot find employment elsewhere, employee is guaranteed a job at (a) no less pay, (b) no "substantial increase in health or safety hazard." (2) Employees given 6 months notice prior to formation of deinstitutionalization plans. (3) Preservation of rights, privileges, and benefits (specifically including pension rights) under existing collective bargaining. (4) Employee training or retraining as necessary. (5) Relocation expenses to employees transferred more than 50 miles from previous employment. (6) Early retirement, if desired, for qualified employees.	Division of Developmental Disabilities, HEW, executes guidelines in conjunction with Department of Labor, to be carried out by the State institutions involved.	State institutions involved.	No substantial cost.

Labor Displacement and Public Policy

Table A-1. Continued

Title	Eligibility	Benefit amount	Duration	Other benefits	Administration	Funding source	Cost
Special Health Revenue Sharing Act of 1975 (Public Law 94-63).	Employees affected by deinstitutionalization of the mentally ill.	No cash benefits.		(1) Training and retraining. (2) Preservation of employee rights and benefits. (3) If dismissed employee cannot find employment elsewhere, employer must find employee a job at same rate of pay and retrain as necessary.	Individual plans administered by State health or mental health authority; Secretary of HEW responsible for ensuring all authorities have fair and equitable protection plan (as determined by Secretary of Labor).	Affected State health or mental health authority.	
1978							
CETA Amendments of 1978 (Public Law 95-524) through Sept. 30, 1982.	Unemployed individual in area of large-scale unemployment with no reasonable expectations of local employment and a bona fide employment offer.	Cash benefits to supplement any UI received up to local minimum wage.	Upon completion of training period.	(1) Relocation loans or grants. (2) Job search assistance.	State agencies or prime sponsors.	Annual congressional appropriations.	
Airline Deregulation Act of 1978 (Public Law 95-504) through Dec. 31, 1989.	Workers with at least 4 years employment with air carrier and laid off by reason of the carrier experiencing a bankruptcy or major contraction (7½ percent or more reduction in full-time employees) caused in major part by this act.	Secretary of Labor in consultation with Secretary of Treasury authorized to determine amount proposed. Regulations provide monthly benefit equal to 70 percent of monthly wages (after Federal income taxes and FICA) paid during recent 12-month period. Current proposed maximum, $1,200 month (66⅔ percent average wage in industry). Reduced by any UI received.	Maximum of 72 months.	Relocation expenses including compensation for loss in selling property or in cancelling lease agreement or contract of purchase. Retention of seniority and recall rights plus first right of hire with other air carriers.	Department of Labor. ETA administers provisions concerning benefit eligibility and amounts, extent of reemployment assistance, and maintaining comprehensive job listing. LMSA administers priority hire rights provisions, air carriers' duties to hire, and negotiations between air carriers and union representatives.	Employee protection account; congressional appropriations.	Not funded.

Legislation	Coverage	Benefit	Duration	Services	Administrator	Funding	Expenditure
Amendment to act establishing National Park (1978) Public Law 95–250 —through Sept. 5, 1984 ("Redwood").	Workers on layoff or down-grading between May 31, 1977, and Sept. 30, 1980, from employer engaged in harvesting or processing redwood timber at park area who: (1) Had collective bargaining determined seniority as of May 31, 1977, and 12-months work as of Mar. 27, 1978, or (2) Had at least 1,000 hours work from Jan. 1, 1977, through Mar. 27, 1978.	100 percent of average pay during 3 of last 5 years in which hours were greatest. Reduced by any wages earned in timber industry and by 50 percent of other wages, social security, and UI. Severance payment option available.	Period equal to length of service, age 65, or June 30, 1984, whichever occurs earliest, except those reaching age 60 before Sept. 30, 1984, remain eligible until 65. Acceptance of optional severance pay (sum equal to total entitlement up to 72 times weekly benefit) ends duration.	Relocation, training, job search benefits, plus continuing entitlement to health, welfare, pension, insurance at no greater cost than when employed.	California Employment Development Department.	U.S. congressional appropriated funds.	$13.9 million as of Dec. 22, 1979.

1979

Legislation	Coverage	Benefit	Duration	Services	Administrator	Funding	Expenditure
Milwaukee Railroad Restructuring Act (1979) (Public Law 96–101) through March 1, 1984.	Workers laid off from the Milwaukee Railroad.	80 percent of average monthly pay between June 1977 and November 1979, less UI and any earnings. May opt for a severance payment not to exceed $25,000.	Period equal to length of service not to exceed 36 months or Apr. 1, 1984.	Career training assistance not to exceed $3,000.	Railroad Retirement Board.	U.S. congressional appropriated funds of $7.25 million.	No funds expended as of yet.
Health Planning and Resources Development Amendments of 1979 (Public Law 96–79).	Workers terminated because of discontinuation of hospital services.	Termination payment only.		Protection against worsening of position, protection of fringe benefits, retraining.	Certification by Department of Labor.	Institutions involved through Federal grants.	No funds expended as of yet.

Source: National Commission on Unemployment Compensation.

Index

About the Author

Philip L. Martin earned the B.A. in economics at the University of Wisconsin-Madison in 1971, and the Ph.D. in economics and agricultural economics from the same university in 1975. Since 1975 he has served on the faculty at the University of California-Davis. In 1978-1979, he was a Fellow at the Brookings Institution in Washington, D.C. In 1979-1980, he was senior economist for the Select Commission on Immigration and Refugee Policy and a consultant to the Department of Labor. His major publications include: *Guestworker Programs: Lessons from Europe* (1980), *Administering Foreign-Worker Programs* (Lexington Books, 1982); and *Contemporary Labor Economics and Labor Relations* (1980).